Invisible Machine Appliqué

Now you and your sewing machine
can create all those lovely,
traditional appliqué designs
you've always dreamed about

*It's easy –
it's fun –
and you can do it!*

TEAMWORK
CRAFTBOOKS

"Dawn Cameron-Dick! Aren't you *somebody?*..."

I think I was born a 'woman of the needle'. I certainly came from a family of very crafty ladies. Although we didn't sit nightly by the open fire and quilt, I was taught to knit, crochet and sew before I reached my teens. Still, I tried many different crafts before the arrival of my first-born, Christopher, in the early 1970s.

It was then that I saw this photo of a Log Cabin quilt and decided, 'Hey! I could make one of those this weekend!' The end result was a 100-block orange and brown quilt which remained at various stages of completion for the next 17 years ... Still, I was well and truly hooked.

A move to Saudi Arabia in 1974 and the birth of my daughter Hollis gave me lots of time to sew. And sew I did! I didn't know how to quilt, so I spent nigh on 7 years piecing tops. Without a rotary cutter or formal patchwork education my results were, to say the least, 'interesting' and varied, but fabric was like a drug to me and I couldn't stop.

The tops mounted up, and in 1980 my British husband Gordon and I decided to leave the Middle East and live in Colorado for a spell. It was here that my Mom and I opened 'Your Fabric Shop' in Castle Rock and I met my friend Judith Baker Montano. She not only taught our beginner classes but also taught me to quilt. About time too!

Quilts eventually were finished and used. Rachel and Alastair were born and still I sewed on. When my husband had the opportunity to take up a position in Belgium we closed our lovely little shop and I flew off into the sunset (or was it sunrise?), thinking that my quilting time was well and truly over. After all, who in *Europe* would be interested in patchwork and quilting? Famous last words...

Above: *opening day for Mum and me in 'Your Fabric Shop,' Castle Rock, Colorado*

Below: *teaching students at home, Waterloo, Belgium*

Within six months of arriving in Waterloo, Belgium, I offered my first beginning class. It ended up being two classes, as the first one filled up in two days. From then on I was teaching an average of four classes a week for the next eight years. I guess I figured that if I was going to be unable to find quilters in Europe I'd just create my own!

And I had some wonderful students. Not just in Belgium but in Luxembourg as well. Quilters who constantly challenged me, surprised me and inspired me. Their never-ending quest for more skills kept me on my toes and forced me to be creative. I can never repay them for helping me become the best teacher I was capable of being.

An exciting class at Quilt Expo '98,
Innsbruck, Austria

Invisible Machine Appliqué was something I had experimented with back in Colorado, but I'd never had the time to explore it fully. The demand from my intermediate students for a Dresden Plate class brought all my ideas back to the surface. From 1988-90 I think I came up with no fewer than two dozen really *FANTASTIC* (in my humble opinion) ideas for preparing appliqué pieces. I now realise that 23½ of them were garbage, but it was a start.

By the time Quilt Expo 92 in Den Haag rolled around my first professional Invisible Machine Appliqué class was accepted and I was invited onto the faculty! The class was well received but still needed work. Two years later I was again invited onto the faculty for Expo 94 in Karlsruhe, Germany. My quilt *Keukenhof* was on display and I had a quilt accepted into the *Hands All Around* Exhibition in Houston, Texas USA. I felt I'd really 'arrived' (especially when a gal at the check-in desk read my badge with quizzical interest and said, 'Dawn Cameron-Dick! Aren't you somebody?' ... *sigh* ...)

The Invisible Machine Appliqué class I taught in Lyon, France (Expo 96) was the finished product pretty much as you see it today. But the ideas never stop coming. Positive responses from students and the ideas they put forth have constantly provided me with the desire and encouragement to go on and do more. And so *Invisible Machine Appliqué Rides Again!* (book 2) is already begun.

Thank you for taking the time to read *Invisible Machine Appliqué*. I hope you enjoy it. I envisioned it as a very personal book so I hope you can excuse the occasional strange turn of a phrase or my rather unusual way of looking at things. I tried to write it as if you were here with me having a class at my kitchen table. I hope the book provides you with a smile and a chuckle now and again. But mostly I hope it informs you and spurs you on to becoming the very best quilter you are capable of being.

Cheers!

*Whatever you can do,
or believe you can do, begin it!
Boldness has genius, power and magic.*

GOETHE

My ability to describe myself as a very happily married lady with four terrific children did not happen without some assistance! Having the unique privilege of living in Saudi Arabia (7 years), Belgium (8 years), England (since 1996) and now part-time in Nigeria didn't come about solely because of my own abilities. And now, finally putting pen to paper and writing this book would never have even been dreamt of as possible without the unfailing belief, support and encouragement of one very special man ...

So I dedicate this book to my best friend, my mentor and the love of my life ... my husband Gordon Cameron-Dick

I also want to say a heartfelt 'thank you' to some very wonderful people:

- **my parents:** *Frank & Lorraine Sobczak* ... married since 1944 and always willing to listen, support, and offer assistance and advice.

- **my children:**

  Christopher M Scoggin – my first born, who single-handedly dragged me into the computer world, thus improving my classes 1000% . Although he and his family live 'across the pond' he is always there for me with amazing insight.

  Hollis Scoggin – my 'Arab Baby,' born in Saudi Arabia on the roadside at dawn. A thorn in my sandal during her infancy but a diamond in my heart as an adult. The beautiful gypsy I could never totally be.

  Rachel Cameron-Dick – the soul of our family. The 'leveller' in my roller-coaster life. Like her sister, as far from being a quilter as one could be, but still 100% respectful of my work. She always has time to listen.

  Alastair Cameron-Dick – the baby of our family, now a man. Artistic, sincere and opinionated. Many of my quilts have benefited from his frank observations and suggestions ... even though they drove me crazy at the time.

- ***And finally, appreciation for those special people who, one way or another, have enriched my life:***

  My lovely mother-in-law, *Dorothy Dick*, who doesn't really understand what I do, but supports me anyway!

  My Aussie daughter *Julie Mountain* – my PA, gourmet cook, dog-walker and comedian. This book would never have been done on time without her.

  Juliet Webster for giving me a start in the UK quilting world.

  Catherine Combe for everything.

  And a big hug to all my multi-national friends and students in Belgium and Luxembourg, who gave me the opportunity to teach and learn at the same time ... especially Clare, Laura, Bridget, Jean, Lena, Hilary and Marianne.

  Also my many new friends here in the UK. The fantastic shops and groups who have welcomed me into their midst with open arms, and the established teachers and professionals who are all so willing to be helpful to the 'new kid on the block'.

Invisible Machine Appliqué
∼ CONTENTS ∼

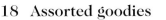
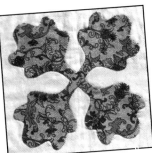

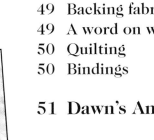

Why *Invisible* Machine Appliqué?

I love hand appliqué. I always have ... even years ago, when I couldn't appliqué anything to save my soul, I jealously revelled in the subtle curves and fluid lines which hand appliqué created. Years of sewing straight, perfect quarter-inch seams left me wanting more flexibility in my designs but, although the heart was more than willing, the fingers seemed unable to cope.

All that preparation! Endless hours of marking, cutting, laboriously turning under seams, tacking (I am sure that is a four letter word!), and still the floppy, soggy piece of fabric had a (malevolent) mind of its own. Gleefully it crept around creating pleats, puckers and a genuine mess.

I considered machine appliqué, but somehow the flatness of bonding web and the intrusive nature of the satin stitch (which, to me, says that this piece of work was definitely not hand-done) just didn't satisfy my needs. Fine, perhaps, for what I call 'artsy-fartsy' quilts, but definitely not at all acceptable for my traditional ones. I became determined to find a better way.

Over the past eight years I've experimented with an infinite combination of stitches, threads, products and techniques in my quest for an acceptable hand-done look. I wanted a technique for anyone who:

    A could not do hand work for some reason

    B disliked doing hand appliqué or

    C simply wanted to get their appliqué done quicker

I was determined to create a traditional-looking appliqué, on the machine, with minimal effort and few – if any – special supplies. Finally, I feel that I have achieved this with **Invisible Machine Appliqué**.

Read on to see if you agree....

Invisible Machine Appliqué

Traditional machine appliqué using satin stitch

Getting Started

❀

Before we look at exactly what Invisible Machine Appliqué (IMA) is, let's cover some of the basics. You're probably already wondering: will I be able to do this technique? Do I need any special skills or equipment? This section should reassure you.

Supplies

In an effort to keep things very simple, I'm pleased to report that you really need only four basic tools to do successful invisible machine appliqué. They are:

Invisible Machine Appliqué: let's call it IMA *for short!*

1 **a sewing machine you really like which:**
- does a blind hem stitch
- is fully adjustable in length and width settings

2 **freezer paper**

3 **spray starch**

4 **a monofilament nylon thread.**
   (Monofilament simply means that there is only one strand in the thread – it isn't made up of several strands twisted together.) I always use YLI Wonder Invisible Thread

In order to 'fine tune' your work there are several things you could make good use of, but they aren't essential:

5 60 or 70 lightweight cotton thread, in a neutral colour, for your bobbin

6 70/10 denim/jeans needles for your machine

7 a small travel iron or a traditional dry iron

8 fine silk pins

9 small, sharp scissors and,

10 for some larger projects, a lightweight, iron-on interfacing

That's not too difficult is it?

Now we'll look at each item in depth, beginning with the most important:

your sewing machine!

Your machine – *love it or leave it!*

~

To be perfectly honest I have two machines. One is a 25-plus-year-old, orange and beige (most fashionable!) Fister Rossmann, which comes in a wee carrying case, can go anywhere with me and cost £50. The other is an older traditional Bernina 1090 (which could never leave my studio without a crane): this cost many piles of £50 notes. I love them both and they both do IMA beautifully. Most machines do.

Below is a check-list of features that I feel are vital in a sewing machine. If your machine scores 5 out of 8 of these features you'll be just fine. (Of course if you want an excuse to go out and buy a new machine, don't let me stop you ... quickly turn to page 6 for advice on how to go about that task intelligently.)

Remember, though, that this is my *very personal pontificating* on sewing machines. Moses most definitely did *not* have these guidelines written on the reverse side of his tablets!

Dream machine check-list

1 Total adjustability on machine stitch length and width

This is most important to any creative machine work. Don't even think about accepting a machine with pre-programmed stitches.

2 Feed dogs that drop to disengage

Covering the feed dogs produces too tight a fit under the pressure foot, and the cover creates a bump which can get in your way – a real problem when free-motion quilting.

3 A blind hem stitch

You're looking for a blind hem stitch which has straight stitches between the 'bites.'

4 Dials rather than button controls

Dials are infinitely more flexible when you want to fine tune a stitch, and you don't get a sore finger from constantly jabbing at a button.

5 A good-sized stitching platform

Some machines give you acres of space, but on some you can feel like a lemming balancing on a cliff! (Still, if you love the machine clear extension tables are often available.)

6 A leg lift

This feature allows you to lift your machine foot with the side of your leg, thus allowing you to keep both hands firmly on your work. There is also a foot pedal available for most machines which will do this job for you if your machine doesn't have the feature built in.

7 The ability to set the machine to stop in the 'needle down' position

Some machines have a button that does this for you, but even some very basic machines can be tricked into it by a firm tap on the foot pedal. This is a most useful feature for doing IMA, and for machine quilting in general. Never again will your work slip a stitch or two when you're not looking! The needle holds everything in place until you're ready to continue sewing.

8 An open-toe appliqué foot

Most machines come with a clear appliqué foot, but I find an 'open-toe' foot preferable for all my IMA and for piecing. It holds the fabric perfectly, but allows you an unobscured view of exactly where your needle is going. If you find this kind of foot difficult to track down you can always adapt your current appliqué foot by simply filing the offending bits off with a metal file; just be sure to smooth the edges very well after filing so that you don't snag your fabrics. What you don't want to use, no matter what your machine or instruction book says, is the blind hem foot: save that for doing real hemming.

Other handy features to look into:

• Just how portable is this machine?
Most machines are described as portable, but in reality go nowhere without a great deal of effort. If you often go to classes and need to be able to pick-up-and-go, you should really insist on carrying the machine around the shop for a while before you make your decision.

• What about the bobbin size?
How much thread the bobbin holds can greatly reduce or increase your sewing time. Berninas traditionally hold quite a lot of thread in their bobbins but I have seen some drop-in bobbins which I don't think would make it through sewing on a binding!

• How accessible is the bobbin?
If the bobbin is in a dark, inaccessible spot you will be wasting a lot of time doing refills. The icing on the cake for any machine is an alarm that warns you when your bobbin is getting low...

• Does this machine have a speed control?
Some machines allow you to set the speed at which you sew (on one brand they denote the slow and fast by using a turtle and a rabbit). This feature is handy when you are a new stitcher, when you're doing very delicate work and when you're teaching a child to sew. Always test the slowest speed of the foot control; the machine should 'creep' at a very slow speed for the best control.

☑ *fully adjustable stitches*
☑ *feed dogs drop*
☑ *does blind hem stitch*
☑ *dial controls*
☑ *large stitching platform*
☑ *leg lift*
☑ *can set in 'needle down'*
☑ *open-toe appliqué foot*
other handy features:

This.....................and not this

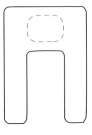 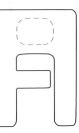

Open-toe appliqué foot   *Standard appliqué foot*

Tips before you buy

Going out to buy a new machine these days can be a daunting experience. If I could give you only one piece of advice about buying a machine it would be:

buy from a local, knowledgeable dealer

This dealer should be an 'authorised stockist' who carries at least six of the twelve makes of machine currently available. Department stores and mail-order companies change brands regularly, and so may not be able to service your machine at a later date.

There will always be the temptation to pick up a bargain or go for a special offer from someone at a quilt show, through a magazine advertisement or while on holiday somewhere. Indeed you may initially be saving some money, but think about these factors:

- **how do you go about getting the machine serviced?**

- **how long will the machine be away for servicing, and who will pay the carriage if it needs to go back to the dealer?**

- **how will you get teaching sessions and advice on the use of your new machine?**

- **will you really have time to 'test drive' the machine at a show before you make your purchase?**

- **will you be able to get a trade-in concession for your old machine?**

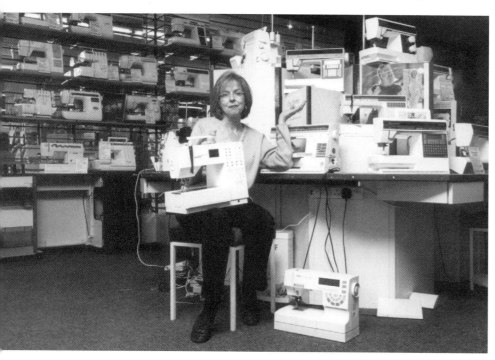

All of these things need to be considered before you can be sure that you're really getting a good deal. I admit that the special offers put out at quilt shows can be tempting, but at these times you're not in the most suitable frame of mind to be making such a major purchase.

I'm sure that dealers across the country aren't going to be very happy with me saying things like this, but the truly good ones will understand my concerns. The best ones will probably be willing to extend the special offer if you make an appointment to visit their shop very soon after the show; that way you can make a more relaxed and educated purchase.

Most stitchers under-utilise their machines by at least 75%

Okay, so that's my own statistic, but it is based upon my experience with hundreds of machines, and their owners, crossing my path.

'In-shop' teaching sessions and a knowledgeable dealer can truly help you get the most out of your investment. A simple test of a shop's helpfulness is to phone them and ask for advice about a mythical stitching problem – 'My thread keeps breaking' or something similar. Their attitude will allow you to judge for yourself how genuinely knowledgeable and helpful they are.

What do you want it to do?

Few of us spend enough time thinking about what we really want a machine to do. When you're sewing one day, why not make a list of all the things you love about your current machine – and then list all the things that drive you batty! Later, sit down with a cup of tea and prioritise the list into must haves and would likes. Make sure that you take this list with you when you go to the shop.

The test drive

Yes, you must sew before you buy!

Would you buy a car simply because the salesman drove it with ease around the showroom forecourt?
I don't think so ... (but if you would, I've got a friend in Denver who would love to sell you a hardly-used Skoda ...)

There's no one 'best' machine, only the one that is best for you, your particular needs and your wallet. Years down the line the bargain price you paid will be long forgotten, but every time you use your machine you'll either be cursing it or blessing it ... which do you want to do?

Any machine will sew well when it's being operated by a seasoned salesman who is sewing on a piece of demo cloth (this is specially-prepared, starched fabric often used to do sales demonstrations): but how will it sew on the fabrics you want to use? The only way to be sure is to try the stitching yourself, on your own fabric. The feel of the machine, the sound of the motor and the size and shape of the foot control are all very personal preferences.

When my mom and I had our shop in Colorado, USA, I was a dealer for Husqvarna/Viking. When a customer came in I asked many questions about what and how she sewed. Then I would put her in the back room with a machine or two of her choice and one of mine. I provided her with different weights of fabric scraps and several different types of thread. I would show her how to thread the machine, pour her a cup of coffee, and then leave her in privacy. Granted it was time-consuming, and I probably didn't sell as many machines as my competitors, but when I made a sale I was darn sure that I had made a perfect match!

I also had a firm policy of refusing to sell a machine to a man for his lady. I would happily provide a gift certificate, but never the actual machine. Think now: would he thank you for choosing his golf clubs, fishing rod or motorcycle for him? I think not!

But so many men seem to think that they know just what's best for their partner ... most likely it's what's best for their bank balance. Just watch their eyes when you calmly explain that a reliable machine, with a life expectancy longer than that of a goldfish, will cost at least as much as an Apex trip for two across the Atlantic. Such a funny, glazed look you will seldom see ...

But I digress. By all means put a machine on your wish list, but specify, in bold print:

GIFT
CERTIFICATE
ONLY!

What to take to the shop

- **your dream machine check-list,** including must-haves and would-likes

- **two rotary-cut 2¹⁄₂in x 40in (roughly) strips of calico.** Press these together, then sew them to see how well they feed through the machine. Do the strips end up even at the end? Does the machine feed straight? (Many don't.)

- **a mini quilt sandwich** (a 10in square of muslin, wadding, and plain top fabric), tacked with safety pins. Use this to test the free-form quilting ability of the machine.

- **a 10in square of dark, plain fabric and a spool of invisible thread** to test the blind hem stitch for IMA. Fold the fabric as shown to form two pleats. Pretend that the pleat is your appliqué fabric.

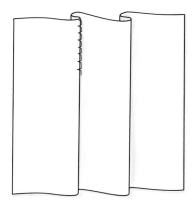

Note: It may be best to leave your credit card home on day one. Any really good deal will still be there tomorrow after a good night's sleep, a rational look at the bank balance and a small rum and coke (optional, granted, but oh, so nice).

Armed with these tools you're prepared to go out and shop ... a well-informed shopper/warrior. For your own sanity try to avoid Saturdays. Go early on your chosen day, and take your time.

GOOD LUCK, SOLDIER!

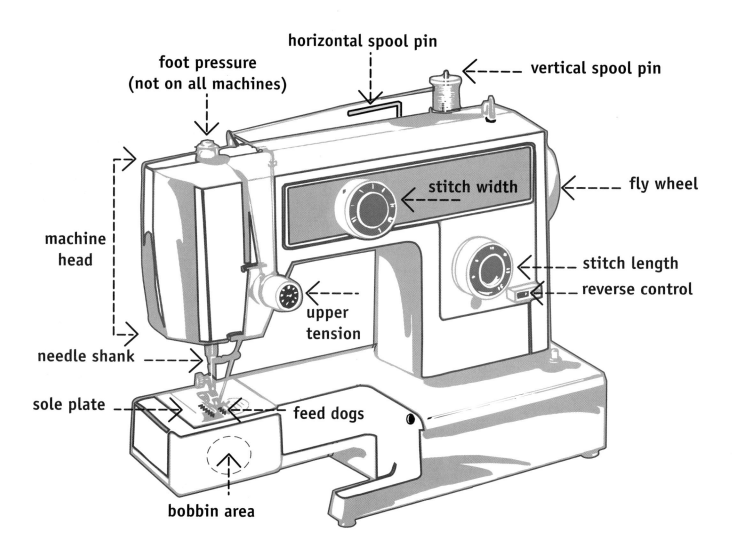

- horizontal spool pin
- foot pressure (not on all machines)
- vertical spool pin
- stitch width
- fly wheel
- machine head
- stitch length
- reverse control
- upper tension
- needle shank
- sole plate
- feed dogs
- bobbin area

Freezer paper

~

'Yes, I have heard about freezer paper, but what is it? And what exactly does it do?' I have heard this question so many times that I'm thinking of having a T-shirt made which reads: 'What *doesn't* it do!?'

I've used freezer paper over the last 15 years for piecing, appliqué (hand and machine), stabilising embroidery and marking quilting designs on my quilt tops. I'm tempted to say that, whatever the question, freezer paper can provide an answer. I love this stuff! God bless the woman who first realised that this product was more useful in the sewing room than in the kitchen. (That applies to *me* as well ...)

What it is ...

Freezer paper is a kitchen product made by the Reynolds Company in America (they are most famous for their aluminium foil). It comes on a roll in a box, much like baking paper or wax paper, but it can't be replaced by either one. It was originally used to package and store meat in the freezer ... hence the name.

The waxy or shiny side of the paper keeps the 'moisture' of the meat from seeping through and making your freezer compartment look like the city morgue after a fight with the Terminator. The paper side allows you to tape it shut and to write '1 lb of mince, 3/3/99' on it. This way, when you pry a white package out from the back of your freezer in several years, you know that it's definitely time to chuck it out. And, as it's so neatly wrapped you'll also keep your dustbin tidy! Now that I have explained things, I won't have to worry about you harbouring the idea of freezer paper being a type of gift-wrap for your deep freeze.

... and what it does

Freezer paper has two sides:

- **the paper side**

This is for writing on. You can draw and erase to your heart's content. Also, as it's fairly light-weight you can easily trace your designs through it. Do get in the habit of drawing with a pencil; if you use a pen and don't cut out within the drawn line, the ink can transfer onto your fabric when you iron it on. Don't even ask how I know this! Spare yourself the grief and use a pencil.

- **the waxy side**

Perhaps waxy is a bad term to use as it's not wax at all but a silicone-based product. It's also important to point out that this shiny side is not an iron-on bonding surface – you don't use freezer paper in the same way that you use something like Bondaweb. It's not permanent and it's not a glue, so if it touches your iron, it won't leave a burnt, gooey mess.

REMEMBER
the waxy side always goes onto your fabric, and you press it on using a hot, dry iron: use the cotton setting.

No matter how you plan to use freezer paper, keep this one fact in mind: *freezer paper is a temporary aid only.* It will always be removed and discarded (that sounds so heartless ...) once it has done its task. Thinking of it this way will keep you from confusing it with iron-on bonding products. Think of it, instead, as a third hand – an indispensable assistant who does a wonderful job then vanishes into the sunset ... and who in all honesty couldn't do with one of those? Pity it doesn't cook!

An emergency substitute for freezer paper

The paper which is used to wrap reams of paper for photocopy machines also has a paper side and a waxy side, and it does work to an extent. The down side is that it's generally a heavier-weight paper. As a result its flexibility is reduced; it's also very hard to trace through , and the paper side often is printed with the name of the manufacturer, which makes drawing difficult. Still, it's free and is readily available; ask your office or local photocopy shop to save it for you. Any port in a storm, I say.

Things that are not freezer paper

Wax paper and baking paper are NOT freezer paper!

- **wax paper**

This is usually beige in colour and has two waxy sides. Useless.

- **baking paper or parchment**

Again, commonly mistaken for freezer paper, but not the same thing at all. Would you substitute salt for sugar just because they look similar? It doesn't work.

Spray starch

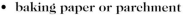

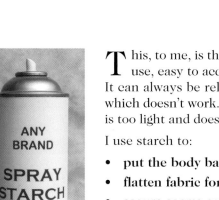

ANY BRAND

SPRAY STARCH

This, to me, is the greatest 'little-known secret' of all quilting time. Easy to use, easy to acquire, inexpensive, and it does wonders for your quilting! It can always be relied upon to do the job, and I haven't yet found a brand which doesn't work. Just be sure to buy spray starch, not 'fabric finish' which is too light and doesn't do a satisfactory job.

I use starch to:

- **put the body back in my fabric after washing**
- **flatten fabric for perfect rotary cutting and machine quilting**
- **secure seams out of the way in preparation for appliqué**

If a choice is available I always choose a heavy-duty starch. (Often people who wear uniforms and need to present a crisp, sharp finish in their clothes know where to get the strongest brand.) You can also buy dried starch, which you mix to the desired strength and then spray on with a plant mister. But I figure that life is already too short without getting into that DIY job!

A word about washing your fabric

Quilters are constantly battling with the 'pre-wash' or 'no pre-wash' question. Many of today's fabrics have a lovely finish, and washing seems to remove that body. Still, if you want to make sure that you avoid any nasty surprises – colour running, shrinkage etc – it's always best to pre-wash. If you get into the habit of washing the fabric as soon as it comes home from the shop you'll always have it ready to use.

You really don't need to clean the fabric; you're simply removing any excess dye and finish that resulted from the manufacturing process. First cut off a ¼in corner at each of the four corners. This does two things:

1 clipping like this prevents the fabric from fraying, which wastes fabric and can cause a nasty, tangled mess in your washing machine

2 missing corners let you know immediately which of your fabrics have been washed. Personally I have fabrics in my stash which are older, by some years, than several of my children. How the heck am I to know if I washed that fabric in 1979 or not?! Still, if the corners are nipped off I know it's safe to use.

Pre-wash your fabrics but put the 'body' back in with the spray starch

Once the fabric is out of the washing machine I either line-dry it to a slightly damp stage, or put it in the dryer for a few moments. From this stage I press it with a hot, dry iron until the fabric is completely dry and then starch it.

Starching

Before spraying on the starch, be sure to shake the can thoroughly (and often). Spray a fine mist all over the fabric, then let it soak in for a moment. This step prevents the irritating tiny white flecks which sometimes mysteriously appear on your fabric.

If you're putting the fabric away for future use, or are planning to use it for hand work, then one spray will be enough. If it's destined for rotary cutting, a few more sprays are in order. The more paper-like it is, the better control you will have. Bias edges won't pull out of line so easily while you're stitching, and fraying in general will be kept at a minimum.

When you're using spray starch for tacking your appliqué seams back (see page 25), I strongly recommend that you first spray the starch into the cap or a small dish. You can then apply it to the fabric exactly where you want it, using a small paintbrush. Spraying it directly onto the appliqué pieces tends to soak the freezer paper, which causes it to wrinkle, and most of the starch is wasted in the air. You end up breathing that air, and it makes your carpet crunch when you walk across it.

If you notice your dog walking around like an Egyptian hieroglyphic, you really must get a dish and paintbrush!

Invisible thread

T his is the real hidden secret of Invisible Machine Appliqué – an absolute godsend. But many years of doing IMA demonstrations at quilt shows have definitely taught me one thing ...

most quilters are not very trusting of invisible thread.

I've heard hundreds of horror stories from quilters. These range from the lady at the National Quilt Championships who had just spent £400 getting her machine repaired after trying to quilt with the brand of invisible thread she had bought at the show the previous year, to a woman who tried to hand-appliqué with one brand and said it was like stitching with a coiled spring! I listen patiently and then try to explain that ...

all invisible threads are not created equal.

Choosing your brand

The difference in brands can be like chalk and cheese. Yes, really! I've seen clear threads that were better suited to pulling caravans or shark-fishing than to our delicate sewing.

Some clear threads are polyester and some are nylon. The one I have used and trusted for over 12 years is the nylon Wonder Invisible Thread made by YLI. It has the feel and thickness of a single strand of human hair. It comes off the spool relaxed and smooth, rather than some threads which come off the spool looking as though they were still on it ... this alone should give you a clue to the thread quality.

The ultimate test of suitability in my opinion is the finger-breaking test. No, not your fingers breaking ... the threads! If you can wrap a single strand between the forefingers of your right and left hands, a simple tug should be enough to break the thread. This doesn't mean that the thread is weak ... simply that it breaks as easily as cotton thread and so is safe to use on our delicate cotton fabrics. The thread strength should always be equal to, or weaker than, the fabric it's sewing. This way, under stress, the sewing thread will break rather than cut through the fabric. You can always re-stitch a broken thread, but how do you mend a cut in the fabric?

Make sure you use a good quality invisible thread

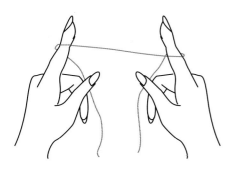

Won't it melt?

Quilters have also questioned the thread's ironability – won't it melt under a hot iron? Even after I've convinced them of the thread's fine feel and its fabric compatibility, logic sets in and the thought arises: 'plastic + heat = a melted mess!' Again I can reassure you. For years I have used, pressed, washed, machine-dried and slept under quilts made using the YLI thread, for both IMA and machine quilting, without ever experiencing a single melt-down.

I thought to myself ... was I exceptionally careful? (Me? Not a chance!) Then maybe I've just been lucky? Again ... not me! (If that black cloud is going to burst I can assure you it will be over my head.) So in order to provide a more professional answer, I contacted YLI direct and learnt that the highest recommended temperature for cotton is 450 degrees Fahrenheit, and YLI's Wonder Thread's melting point is even higher. Now, realistically, when was the last time you scorched your fabric? Since we're all reasonably sensible people, this thread will meet and probably exceed our expectations.

Other practicalities

The distinctive YLI spool also deserves mention. It's lightweight, the paper on the bottom leaves no gooey residue if removed and, as it's wider at the base than at the top, the smooth thread isn't likely to shimmy off the spool as you sew and wrap itself around your spool pin. This happens quite often with other invisible threads, and with some slippery rayon and metallic threads. The YLI design helps avoid this, and thus the 'spin-back' and skipped stitches that result.

The spool also holds over 1500 yards! I have found that I either lose or give away my spools long before I ever manage to empty them. The thread is available in clear and smoke but I generally use the clear. I've had trouble trying to imagine what type of thing I'd be sewing which would require the smoke thread. Perhaps a raven flying in a night sky? On light fabrics I feel that it leaves a shadow next to the appliqué.

Some people find threading the needle difficult with invisible thread. If you have this problem, try putting a dot on the tip of the thread using a black permanent felt-tip marker. Or simply pull some extra thread down after threading the machine, remove the needle, thread it (right) and replace the needle already threaded. There's more than one way to skin a cat ...

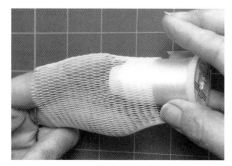

If you have a problem keeping the thread wound on the spool, there's a fine mesh 'sleeve' available that fits snugly over the spool; you feed the thread through it.

The mesh also keeps the spool tidy in your sewing box.

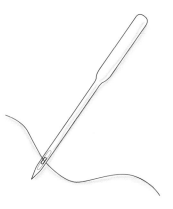

Threads and needles

~

Now a word about sewing machine needles and thread ... or, the birds and the bees of sewing!

I've found over the years that even the most accomplished quiltmakers seem to have huge, gaping holes in their basic knowledge of needles and thread. If this seems to describe you, please don't be embarrassed as you are only one of many who have been let down by the sewing industry. It's my personal theory that home sewing and dressmaking began to go into a decline about the same time as polyester came into existence as a thread and as fabric. It then just became more cost-effective for thread manufacturers to offer the dwindling numbers of stitchers an ever-smaller selection of options.

At one time you went into a shop and asked for 'red cotton, 50 weight' and you got cotton-fibre thread, in the colour red, and of a weight suitable for sewing medium-weight cotton fabrics. Today you ask for 'red cotton' and you will probably be presented with a spool of supposedly 'all-purpose' polyester thread. If you're lucky it may even be red!

The term all-purpose is misleading to an extent. As I said about invisible threads: all threads are not created equal. There is a correct thread for every purpose, and the best results are achieved when there is a happy union between fabric, thread and needle.

Threads

~

Cotton thread comes in many sizes:

100 wt, 70 wt, 60 wt, 50 wt, 40 wt, 30 wt

And each size has a specific sewing job that it does best.

The larger the number the finer the thread. 100 wt cotton thread is very fine, and perfect for lace or heirloom sewing. 40 wt is what our quilting thread generally is, and 50 wt is the standard thread we use for piecing.

Examine a spool of good-quality thread and you should see the following information:

- the *fibre* content (eg cotton, cotton/polyester, polyester)
- the *weight* (eg 50 wt). Polyester threads are not described by weight. If there's a number after the weight, eg 50/3, it tells you how many threads are twisted together.
- the *length* (the number of yards or metres on the spool)
- the *colour number* or maybe a colour name (necessary for future matching)

With this information you can make a well-informed purchase. The more information a manufacturer gives me, the more confident I can be of the thread's quality. Without it you're buying the proverbial pig in a poke: it could be anything! A well-known brand name doesn't necessarily guarantee good results. It can simply indicate good marketing, or an old track record which may no longer provide the quality it once did. You must make your own educated decision.

For general sewing always match your top and bobbin threads. For IMA use nylon on top and fine cotton in the bobbin.

How do I determine the quality of a thread?

Cut a short piece of the thread and hold it up to a dark wall or curtain. Does it look like a Cairn Terrier having a bad hair day (left)? All that hairy stuff is a sure sign of a thread made with a lesser-quality cotton, and is possibly also a sign of shoddy manufacturing standards. This fluff is what helps create some of that lint which constantly needs to be cleaned out from your lovely machine (cotton fabric itself creates the rest of it).

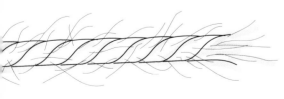

Now twist the thread back and forth between your fingers. Does it unravel easily? If so, it's a weak thread which can't be relied on to hold your precious quilt together for the next 100 years! It will also be a nightmare to thread, which could well make you look 100 years old ... you have been warned.

A quality thread is smooth, even and tightly spun. It may cost a bit more, but the absence of skipped stitches, broken threads and puckering seams is well worth a few pennies, in my book.

Perhaps this is the time to explain just what it is I have against polyester thread ...

Just about everything!

Polyester is too strong for our cotton quilts. The thread won't break when stressed: instead it can cut through your seams. I can always re-stitch a broken seam, but repairing a cut seam is just too depressing to think about. Also polyester, like all plastic, shrinks from heat. Ever put a plastic cup too close to the kettle and ended up with a remarkable work of modern art? As quilters we need to press, press and press again as we assemble our quilts. Every time we do this the heat from the iron causes the polyester thread to shrink just a bit. No wonder some people just can't seem to get a flat-looking seam; it may be the choice of thread.

Points to remember when buying

I buy my thread in bulk; either very large spools, or many boxes at once. When you're making bulk purchases you could politely ask for a small discount. You are buying many spools and giving the shop a good quick turnover on their stock: money changes hands, and you become a satisfied customer most likely to return.

I feel that there is no need to match your thread colour to your fabric, either when you're piecing or when you're doing IMA, so I always buy a neutral beige or white. I fill lots of bobbins at once, which saves time when I'm sewing.

Another thought on colour: my dear old friend Judith Baker Montano (who was my first and only quilt teacher, even though I met her eight years after beginning to make quilts ...) suggested using a mid-grey, as it was a shade that easily blended with most colours. My only problem with this is that I use a lot of 'lights' in my work and the grey seemed too dark for me. If you use a lot of medium and dark shades of fabric, a medium grey may be just the right choice for you.

Remember that, except in very special cases (eg with nylon or metallic novelty threads), your top and bobbin threads should be the same. Resist that urge to grab any old bobbin in your box 'just to use it up.' In fact, why not dedicate one cold evening to emptying all those half-filled bobbins? Yes, it is completely legal and moral to remove the thread and throw it away. Threads get old too. Think of this as sending the thread to a far, far better place. May it rest in peace – you and your bobbins are now free!

Always buy the best thread you can afford and think twice about using polyester.

Below you'll find a chart showing the best combinations of threads and needles; feel free to photocopy this and keep a copy in your handbag or your workbox

THREAD TYPE: (• possible choice ☆ best choice)	NEEDLE SIZE:	60/8	70/10	75/11	80/12	90/14	100/16	topstitch
nylon monofilament ☆ YLI wonder thread		•	☆	•	•	–	–	–
fine machine emb. thread ☆ 60/2 Mettler; ☆ YLI Heirloom 70/2		–	☆	•	–	–	–	–
cotton 50/3 Sylko; Coats; Mettler; ☆ YLI Select		–	–	•	☆	–	–	–
polyester not recommended for patchwork projects		–	–	•	•	•	–	–
cotton-wrapped polyester		–	–	–	–	•	•	–
rayon & metallic (low resistance to abrasion, so not suitable for items intended for heavy wear); ☆ YLI Metallic		–	•	• embroidery	☆ metallica needle	–	–	90/14 •
YLI Jean Stitch		–	–	–	–	–	–	90/14 •
DMC pearl cotton no8		–	–	–	–	–	–	100/16 •

Bobbin threads: use matching thread in your bobbin except with monofilament; then use 100% cotton.
YLI Lingerie and Bobbin is good to use with metallic threads.

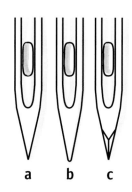

Needles

~

Machine needles come with different kinds of point for different stitching tasks.

*Diagram **a** shows the conventional point; **b** shows a ball-point needle (useful for knit fabrics), and **c** has an extra-sharp chiselled point (used for thick fabrics such as denim and leather).*

There are no exceptions to this rule:

buy the best you can afford, and avoid multi-size packages.

Remember, too, that sewing machine companies don't make needles specially for their machines; they simply set up a deal with the needle manufacturer, and put their name on the package. Don't let the salesperson for your 'Susie Stitcher' machine con you into purchasing only 'Susie Stitcher' needles. All domestic sewing machines made since the Second World War use the same flat-backed, long-shank needles. The difference comes in the quality of manufacture: you get what you pay for. Even the most exotic, speciality needles shouldn't cost you more than a can of soft drink each, and will greatly increase your sewing satisfaction. So why skimp?

How do I know which needle to use?

Size: sewing machine needle sizes go from low (= fine), to high (= heavy-duty). This is in direct opposition to hand-sewing needles, where a no12 between is finer than a no9 between. Who came up with this lunacy? Undoubtedly a man, and he must have been a close relative of the voltage guy who came up with 110 for the USA, 220 for continental Europe and up to 240 for the UK!

Here's a rough guide to which needles to use for what. You'll see that there are two different numbering systems. The first number is the metric size, and the second is the imperial, but the same principle holds true for both: the smaller the number, the finer the needle.

90/14	80/12	70/(11)10	60/8
denim	general medium	fine cottons	lawn/batiste
heavy cottons	cottons		

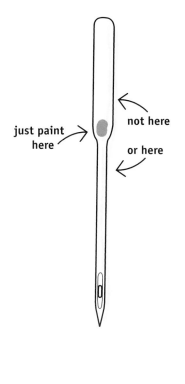

just paint here → not here or here

Needles are stamped with their number at the top, but you generally need a microscope to read it. Why not get some bottles of funky, cheap nail varnish in, say, blue, yellow, green and red and paint the top of each needle with a different colour depending on its size. Just be sure only to put a tiny dot of colour on the needle, and only in the area shown. Let the paint dry fully. If you put it any higher, varnish could accumulate in the needle bar and prevent the full insertion of the needle. Now put a matching blob of varnish on the package. Not only will the needles be easier to identify, but the girl at the cosmetics counter will think you're really cool ...

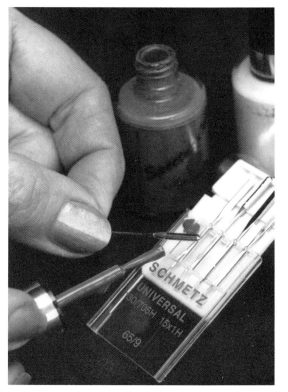

Machine needles for quilters

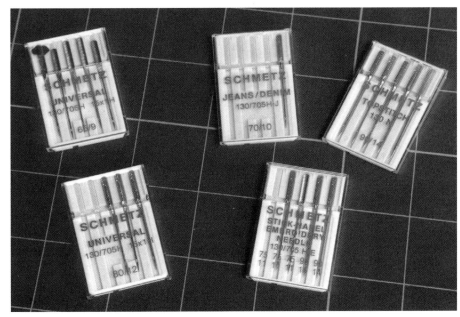

• Universal

In reality this needle is anything but universal. It's a needle that does many jobs adequately but none exceptionally; it's most probably the needle now in your machine.

Universal needles usually come in multi-size packages of five: two 90/14s, two 80/12s and one 70/10. This is a wasteful way to buy needles, as you seldom use 90/14s yet can often go through 80/12s like grass through a goose.

• Quilting

A new, somewhat expensive addition to the machine needle world. The quilting needle has a tapered point, and the eye itself is coated in Teflon; this is intended to decrease the friction of the thread passing through the eye so quickly and for such extended periods. Schmetz quilting needles are coloured green for easy identification, and come with sizes 75/11 and 90/14 in the package.

*Check your needle.
A 70/10 is best with
invisible thread.*

• Denim/jeans

The sharpest needle made. Its name makes you assume that it's only for sewing heavy denim or hemming jeans, but actually it comes in several sizes from 70/10 to 110/18. Its sharp, tapered point stabs heartily into the fabric, deposits the thread and creates a beautiful stitch with no damage to the fabric.

The Schmetz version has a blue band on the upper shaft so you can easily identify it – even without nail varnish! It has become the needle de jour for myself and numerous well-known quilters. You need needles anyway, so why not give these a try?

• Top-stitch

This usually comes in a 90/14 size; it's made for sewing with heavier-weight threads such as YLI Jean Stitch. Great if you want a bold line or to highlight particular parts of your design. The elongated eye also helps with metallic thread, but even better is …

• Metallica

This needle is specially designed for sewing with metallic threads, which are traditionally prone to shredding and breaking. The needle has a deeper shaft than usual so that the thread doesn't fray as it goes into the eye. An absolute necessity when sewing with metallic threads.

• Embroidery

Another good 'work-horse.' Great for rayon threads and the assorted unusual-but-yummy threads available for machine embroidery. Most useful in 90/14 size.

Assorted goodies

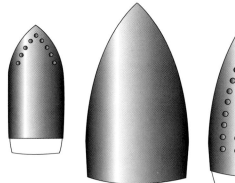

Irons

I found a wee travel iron which I really enjoy using. I use it dry, and as it's practically the size of my hand I feel I have more control when pressing curves and dips. Available for around a tenner, a little travel iron like this can do double duty on holiday and in classes.

The other good option would be a dry iron. Steam irons have those annoying holes on the sole-plate which always seem to catch on my fabric. With a dry iron there are no holes, and so I feel I have much more control over where my fabric goes as I press. Look for a smallish one for easier handling.

Above, left to right: *travel iron, dry iron, standard iron*

Scissors

Once again, invest in the best you can find. Buy a large 8in pair for larger cuts, and a small embroidery size for cutting threads and clipping seams. Check that they have a screw at the join so that they can be tightened as they age. When you're using scissors you have most control at the point, so the blades must meet very well. The handles should be comfortable around your fingers, and most importantly the scissors should cut cleanly and right to the tip. A good investment should last a lifetime. If you're left-handed, remember that you can buy scissors to suit your southpaw leanings.

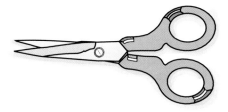

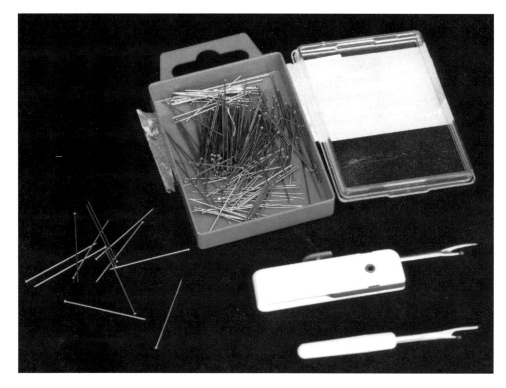

Silk pins

When I'm teaching classes I'm prone to pinching students' tools rather than toting around my own. Generally that works fine, except in the case of pins: most pins I come across would be put to better use for picture hanging. Fat, stubby and dull are all descriptions which come to mind: these bullies make holes in your fabric, and worst of all end up distorting the very seams they are meant to keep in line.

Silk pins, usually a size 13mm-04, are elegant, slim and wonderfully sharp. Treat yourself and find some today, then put them in a nice box and protect them from the likes of me!

Seam ripper

(Or a 'reverse sewing machine,' as some people like to call it!) Using the tips of scissors or a blade is very unpredictable, to say the least. Get one that looks like those pictured above.

Beginning Invisible Machine Appliqué

❖

Now let's get down to the nitty gritty ...

Preparing your machine for IMA

1 Be sure the machine is clean.
Remove the sole plate and, with a soft brush, clean out all that cotton lint; then oil the machine. Most modern machines don't need oil in the head, just a drop or so on the bobbin. Don't overdo the oil: usually just a drop of a good-quality sewing machine oil will do – check in your instruction manual. In this instance, less can actually be better than more.

After oiling, run the machine for a few minutes on scrap fabric. Oil has been known to sneak onto the bobbin thread, and this can cause a nasty oily stain, especially on light-coloured fabrics. Always sew at full speed for at least a minute after oiling ... or live to regret it!

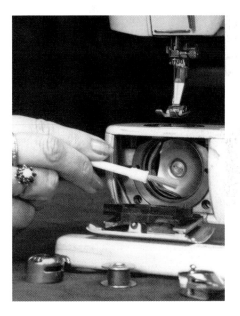

2 Fill your bobbin with a lightweight (60wt or 70wt) cotton thread in a neutral colour.
Choose a neutral shade unless you are stitching all dark fabrics – then a mid-grey is good. If you can't locate 60 or 70 use your usual 50wt, but be sure that it's a good-quality cotton.

3 Thread your machine with the same thread on top.
You aren't going to IMA just yet: first of all, I want to be sure that your stitch is correct.

4 Prepare a 10in square of dark, plain fabric (see p8) by pressing in two pleats.

5 Now check your manual to see how to set your machine for blind hemming.
The stitch looks like this ⎯⎯⎯∨⎯⎯∨⎯⎯∨

It's commonly available on most machines; it's intended for stitching nearly invisible hems on clothes and curtains.

Adjust the settings of your machine as recommended for the blind hemming stitch, but, no matter what the manual suggests, do not put the recommended blind hem foot on your machine. The blind hem foot has a blade running down the centre which causes the thread to be thrown over; as a result it's less likely to snap under stress (I wonder if they make one for people?)

• *If you don't have this stitch on your machine, you may have one which looks like this:* ⋀⋀⋀⋀⋀⋀⋀

It's not an ideal choice, but we may be able to make it look presentable for IMA depending on just how much your machine will allow you to adjust your stitch length and width.

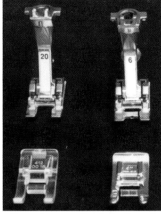

Open-toe appliqué foot and other standard appliqué feet: fine to use

Blind hemming foot: do not use

You could use your normal multi-stitch foot at this point, but an open-toe appliqué foot is better; for Bernina machines it's no20. Or try using your clear appliqué foot. That bar across the ordinary foot is fine for general sewing, but in appliqué it's like driving with a plank of wood attached to the front of your bonnet!

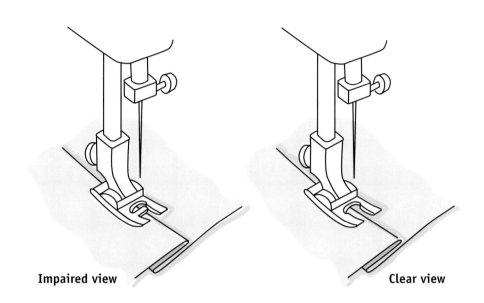

Impaired view　　　　　　　　　　　　　　　　　　　　**Clear view**

Starting to stitch

1 Place your prepared fabric square on your machine with the first fold on the left.

The slit on your pressure foot should be in line with the edge of the fold, or, if you're using an open-toe foot then make sure that the right-hand toe is running against the fold (Unless you have a Husqvarna/Viking machine, your machine will probably 'bite' to the left. The Husqvarna bites the other way so simply place your appliqué piece to the right of the needle.)

2 Stitch half-way down your fold.

The stitch will be large: `‒‒‒∨‒‒‒∨‒‒‒`

That's fine, as I want you to see how the stitch is formed and get comfortable with keeping straight stitches on the background and the bites on the fold. Now is the time to count the straight stitches between your 'bites' (the little V-shaped bits). There will probably be four or five. This information will be helpful once you actually begin appliquéing.

3 Now stop sewing and reduce your stitch *length*; `‒‒∨‒‒∨‒‒∨`

try 1.5 to begin with. Stitch to the end of the row.

4 Go to the top of the next fold and reduce your *width*:

again try 1.5. Your stitch should look like this: `‒‒∨‒‒∨‒‒∨`
Use the narrowest 'bite' you can comfortably see.

Now for the vanishing act...

1 Change to the nylon thread on top.

Keep the lightweight cotton on the bobbin, and make sure that you're using your open-toe appliqué foot.

Use nylon on the top and cotton on the bottom. Reduce length and width to about 1.5. An open-toe foot is helpful.

You are now ready to try real IMA!

REMEMBER
The straight stitches are only on the background fabric, immediately next to the folded edge of the appliqué. Only the bites will touch the appliqué. Even if your machine stitches with the double zigzag, you must reduce your stitches to keep the 'zigs' small and away from the appliqué.

2 Stitch down your second fold. Stop if you are seeing too much bobbin thread ('snow,' I call it) on the top of your fabric. To get rid of the snow try reducing your upper tension. The lower the number on the dial the less the upper thread pulls on the bobbin thread; try not to go much below the number 2 on the dial.

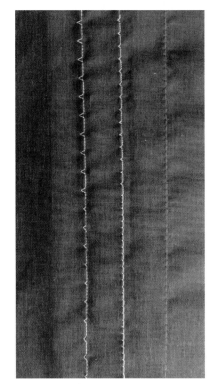

If the bobbin thread still shows, you can try the following:

- have you used a fine bobbin thread, 70 or 60 weight?

- Bernina owners can put the bobbin thread through the tiny hole at the end of the bobbin casing 'finger'.

- have you used a 70/10 needle?

- tighten the bobbin screw a tiny bit. Always move in very small increments to the right, and remember to loosen the screw again by the same amount when you return to normal sewing.

Once you are happy with the look of your stitches, we can be more adventurous. After all, you won't always be appliquéing straight lines!

If possible, set your machine in the 'needle down' mode (see p5); this will help to keep your work from slipping on curves.

REMEMBER
Stitch slowly at first. You counted your straight stitches, so you will know when to expect a bite; this means you'll be able to position it exactly where you want it.

Appliquéing points and curves

~

At this stage we'll just talk about the theory of how to deal with points and curves, but soon you'll be actually stitching them.

• points

As you approach a point, pay close attention to your straight-stitch count and work to make sure your needle will bite on the tip of the point.

This area of an appliqué is very delicate, and you must make sure that you secure it firmly. If you're getting close and are afraid your count will over-shoot the point (**a**), simply hold the background fabric with your right hand and exert a gentle resistance to the feed dogs' efforts to move the fabric forwards. You will then have a small build-up of straight stitches. Now you can allow the fabric to move and bite only when you are actually at the correct position (**b**).

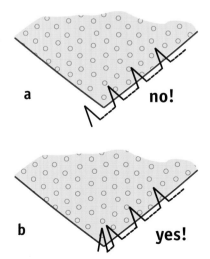

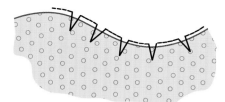

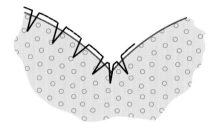

• deep curves

In the 'needle down' position it's easy to manoeuvre curves as you simply sew some straight stitches, stop with the needle down, lift the pressure foot a bit, and ever-so-slightly turn the work. Even without the 'needle down' option you can try tapping the foot pedal to guide the needle down, or simply do it manually with the fly wheel.

• dips

Dips are handled much the same as deep curves, except that you're going to try and put a few more bites in the dip itself; again this is a delicate area, apt to fray, and it needs the security of being anchored with a few extra bites. Don't worry about the thread building up and causing a rough edge; if you have used a top-quality invisible thread, the edge will remain soft and pliable no matter how many extra stitches you lay down.

Finally ...

To finish stitching I simply stitch over about ¼in of the beginning stitches. I watch out for a bite count of three straight stitches, push the reverse button after the last one, and make a final two straight stitches in reverse. This seems to lock and secure the ends very well. Clip your ends very close to the fabric.

Your machine now knows how to do the appliqué stitch.
The only thing left is to show YOU how to
prepare the appliqué pieces.

*The heart here is stitched with **black** thread rather than nylon thread so that you can see the stitching easily.*

Preparing your fabric for appliqué

~

I feel the main reason that this method looks so much like real hand appliqué is that it has **turned under edges!** Appliqué done with bonding web or satin stitch produces hard edges that immediately catch the eye and announce to the world that this has not been done by hand. When stitching by hand we can gently coax the seam allowances under and stitch them down; unfortunately, though, our machines are not yet capable of doing this manoeuvre, so we must first prepare the appliqué pieces.

Over the years I've tried many different ways of turning under those edges, and have now narrowed it down to the following four methods. Some people always use just one method, but I find that different sizes and shapes of appliqué pieces require the use of different preparation techniques. Try them all and see which you like the best.

Four methods for preparing your shapes for IMA

I suggest that you prepare four heart shapes, one in each method, and appliqué them onto a square of plain fabric. Then with a pen you can note next to each one how it was prepared, and also your personal notes and feelings about each method. Tuck this sample square into the back of this book, and you have a permanent record of your experiences. (You could try a Drunkard's Path block – see page 37 – as shown in the bottom right-hand corner of the sample above.)

To do this you will need:

- [ ] one 10in square of plain background fabric
- [ ] six 5in squares of fabric for the shapes
- [ ] three 5in squares of freezer paper
- [ ] one 5in square of featherweight iron-on interfacing (eg Vilene)
- [ ] your sewing machine
- [ ] spray starch and paintbrush
- [ ] a pencil
- [ ] scissors and pins
- [ ] an iron
- [ ] invisible thread and cotton thread

❧ Method 1 ❧
Freezer paper and spray starch

1 Trace the heart shape below directly onto the paper side of the freezer paper. (Remember to use a pencil for this. If you use a pen and don't cut out exactly on the line, you could leave some ink on the paper; this could end up being transferred onto your fabric, which would most likely make you somewhat cranky.)

2 Cut out the heart on the drawn line. This is the finished size of the appliqué.

3 Place your fabric on the ironing board wrong side up.

4 Set your iron on the cotton setting, and turn off the steam. Steam only makes the paper wet, and we don't need that! First press the fabric to warm it up a bit; I find that this really helps the paper to stick.

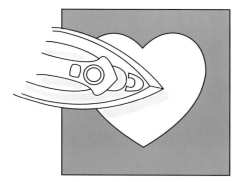

5 Now place the freezer paper appliqué shiny side on the fabric, and press. Don't slide the iron around; instead just exert a bit of pressure and let the heat do the work. Six seconds should be adequate. Once you remove the iron, let the piece cool for a moment and then your freezer paper heart will be firmly stuck to the fabric.

You have now accomplished three things:
- **The shape has been put on the fabric without needing to actually mark on the fabric. This is very useful when you are trying to mark on dark fabrics, and on light fabrics there are no pencil marks.**
- **You have stabilised the fabric so it won't fray or pull off-grain.**
- **You have given yourself a firm edge around your desired appliqué shape to guide you as you turn your seam allowances under.**

❧❧❧ Pros and cons

✓ perhaps the most-used method

✓ very good for medium-size pieces

✗ note that your design will be reversed with this method

You draw this: You appliqué this:

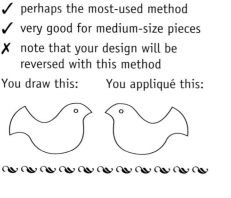

❧❧❧❧❧❧❧❧❧❧❧

 If you look and the paper heart has vanished, try looking at the underside of your iron. Chances are that it's firmly stuck to the sole plate because you positioned it wrong side up. Don't feel bad; we've all done it at least once – some of us many more times than we care to admit. It won't harm the iron. Just pull the piece off and try again: REMEMBER, shiny side always goes to the fabric!

Turning under the seam allowance

At this point you could turn the seams back and hand-tack them in place with a needle and thread. You also could repaint your house using a toothpick, but there are easier ways. All you need is a can of spray starch, two small cheap paintbrushes (pinch them from your kids ... after all, they're always stealing your stuff!), and a small dish of water.

a Spray some of the spray starch into the cap. The foam will soon vanish and leave in its place liquid starch.

b Use one of your brushes and paint a quarter-inch of starch all around your heart, still on the wrong side of the fabric. It will be easy to see where you've put the starch as it darkens the fabric.

c Now cut the fabric heart out around the freezer paper allowing a scant ¹/₄in seam allowance.

d Take the slightly damp heart to the ironing board and, using the tip and side of the iron, gently roll the wet seam allowances over the freezer paper. Begin in the long straight area and work your way up to the curves at the top of the heart.

e You'll need to make three small clips into the area between the humps at the top as shown (bottom and right). Work slowly at first, until you get the hang of the technique.

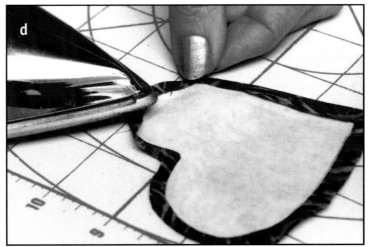

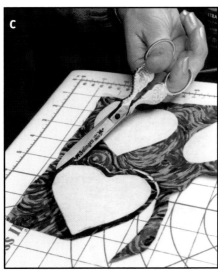

f Work your way carefully downwards from the top edge, along the straight side of the heart and towards the tip.

g Press the tip of the heart by folding over and pressing first one edge and then the other, as shown in the diagrams; this gives you a neat, sharp point.

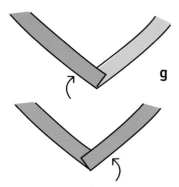

Press each part of the seam until the starch is dry and your seam allowances are firmly held in place. They won't be sticky or stiff, and there are no tacking threads to remove. What you do have are the seam allowances held to the back, and a firm edge for your machine to appliqué against. And all in less time than it would have taken me to thread the needle to hand-tack!

Problem solving

Sometimes the seams just do not press exactly where you want them – a pleat forms. Or a dip doesn't press back as well as you would like ... any number of things can go amiss. Don't worry! Water comes to the rescue. If you keep a spare paintbrush and a wee dish of water handy you can simply brush a bit of water on the dry, nasty seam. Open the seam and use your fingers to flatten it out; now re-press the seam into the correct position.

(Dare I mention that this can also be done with a little bit of spit on your fingers? Either way it's a very easy way to correct your mistakes.)

With larger shapes (eg, *Antique Oak* on page 76), I paint and press as I go; if I paint the entire design, parts usually dry before I get there to press them over. Even so, a dab of water rehydrates them in just the same way.

❧ METHOD 2 ❧
Freezer paper shiny side up

1 On the paper side of the freezer paper, draw your design as you wish it to appear. (At the moment you're working on the heart shape, which is symmetrical, but this method will not reverse a directional design.)

2 Cut the shape out along the drawn line.

3 Place your fabric, **wrong side up**, on your ironing board, and pin the freezer paper shape to it, making sure the waxy side is facing you.

4 Carefully cut the shape out, allowing an ample ¼in seam allowance all round (**a**).

5 Clip the inside curves.

6 Put the shape you're pressing on a firm surface and, using just the side edge of a hot, dry iron, gently press the seam allowance onto the wax surface (**b**).

REMEMBER:
It isn't really wax and won't hurt your iron.

Don't panic if you make a mistake. Simply pull up the fabric and re-iron it in position.

An added benefit of this technique is that you can now iron your prepared appliqué shape onto your background to hold it in place for stitching!

Pros and cons

✓ good for very simples shapes

✓ doesn't reverse your design

You draw this: You appliqué this:

✗ can be difficult to use on very tiny or complicated shapes

a

A brief word about clipping seams. Inner curves need help; outer curves will roll over if the seam allowance isn't very large. Repeat after me: 'you only CLIP in the DIP, never on the HUMP.'

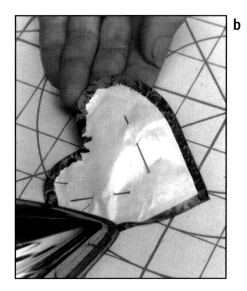

b

Method 3
Lining with iron-on interfacing

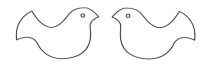

Pros and cons

✓ great for medium-to-large pieces

✓ excellent for shapes with seams (eg Dresden Plate or Crown of Thorns) which make them too bulky for freezer paper pressing

✗ your design will be reversed when appliquéd

You draw this: You appliqué this:

Method 3 is the best one for appliquéing designs which have already been pieced, such as the New York Beauty and Dresden Plate shown below

1 Make a plastic or cardboard template of your shape (in this case, of course, you're using the same heart shape as for method 1, page 24).

2 Use a pencil to draw round the template onto the wrong side of your fabric (**a**).

3 Place the featherweight iron-on interfacing with its soft (non-glue) side to the right side of your appliqué fabric (**b**). The rough or bumpy side is the fusible side which carries the glue, and that side should be against your machine when you sew. (It's easy to get this wrong, with disastrous results. I always try to remember 'nice to nice': nice soft side of the fusible interfacing to the nice pretty side of the fabric.)

4 The wrong side of the fabric, with your drawing on it, should be facing you now, and you will sew completely around this shape. Stitch with regular cotton thread in your machine, and use the shortest stitch your machine can comfortably sew (**c**). Try a 0.5; you should barely be able to distinguish one stitch from the other. On my machine the stitches look like a tiny string of pearls. Just don't let the machine jam up or choke on the stitches; the stitches should be small, but the needle should still be moving forward!

5 Now for the scary part. You will need to trim the seams down to about $1/16$ in (**d**) which, in less technical terms, is about the width of your large scissors blade. Do be careful, but don't be afraid. You have stitched a very strong seam, and the stitching will keep the fabric secure.

6 As you have stitched completely around the shape, the only way to turn the piece right side out is to make a small opening in the fusible interfacing. Depending on the shape I've sewn I usually make an X or a slit (**e**). Be sure to cut only through the interfacing and not your appliqué fabric!!

7 Gently turn the appliqué shape right side out. Don't cut away any of the interfacing just yet.

8 Place the shape on your ironing board with the fabric side down. Carefully pull on the interfacing so that just a thread or two of the appliqué fabric begins to show on the back, then press the edge of the interfacing with your hot, dry iron (**f**). This secures your seam to the back of your piece, and no fusible interfacing will show on the front edge of your work.

9 I generally only press down about $1/4$ in of the interfacing and then cut away the rest (**g**). This way I have only a small amount remaining around the edges; my appliqué piece stays soft and flexible, and there will be no added bulk to interfere with my quilting.

When you're sewing a pieced unit (eg a Dresden Plate), simply lay the unit right sides together with the fusible interfacing and sew your tiny stitches a scant $1/4$ in from the edges. (I say scant because there's always something lost in the turning and, if you have points to protect, the 'scant' seam ensures that they stay sharp.) Then trim the seam very close (left), turn out and press the piece as instructed above, again leaving only $1/4$ in of fusible interfacing pressed to the reverse side of the unit.

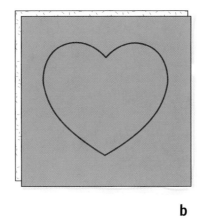

a

b

c

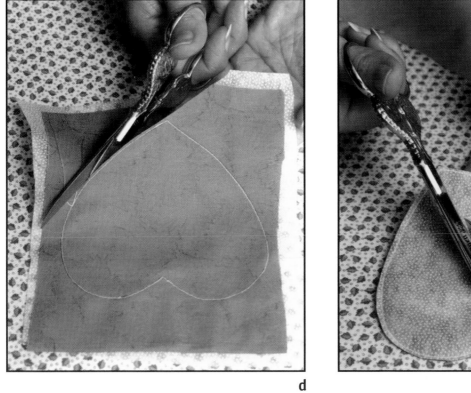

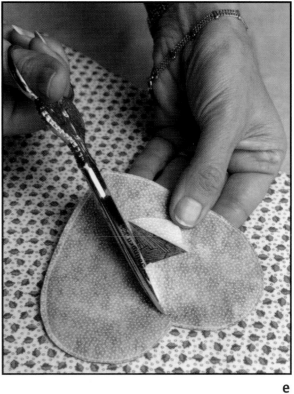

d

e

f

g

❧ METHOD 4 ❧
Lining with fabric

ᔥ ᔥ ᔥ ᔥ ᔥ ᔥ ᔥ ᔥ ᔥ ᔥ ᔥ ᔥ

Pros and cons

✓ necessary when you wish to keep any part of your design three dimensional

✗ requires extra good-quality fabric

ᔥ ᔥ ᔥ ᔥ ᔥ ᔥ ᔥ ᔥ ᔥ ᔥ ᔥ ᔥ

1 Follow the directions for Method 3 (see page 28), but replace the fusible interfacing with a piece of the same fabric that you're using for the front of your appliqué.

It isn't necessary to cut the backing as most likely this piece will be inserted into something and so will have an open edge. (For example, the ears on a rabbit which would be inserted behind the piece used for its head.)

2 After you've turned the unit right side out, you'll still press the lining fabric to the wrong side of the work, but of course it won't adhere as it does with fusible interfacing. A short spray of spray starch helps the seams stay in place.

3 (When working on an actual piece rather than your trial heart): place the lined piece between the background and the piece which it is inserted into. Pin the pieces carefully, and appliqué stitch over the join.

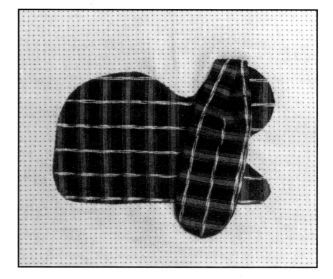

METHODS 1-4
Samples of each method

Whatever kind of appliqué project you're doing, you'll most likely find that one of the four methods I've shown you is a perfect way of preparing your fabric pieces ready to stitch. I use all the methods in my work, as you can see from the details below – all the samples are taken from the project section of this book.

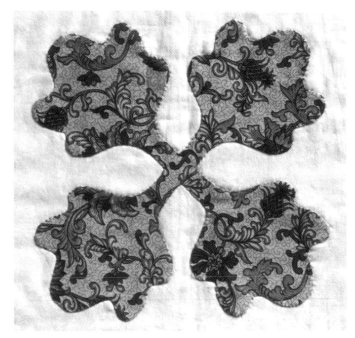

METHOD 1 *was used to prepare the pieces for* Antique Oak *(see page 76)*

METHOD 2 *was perfect for the pieces that build into* Country Hearts *(see page 57)*

METHOD 3 *is useful for appliquéing sections that have already been pieced, such as the* Dresden Plate *(see page 81)*

METHOD 4 *allowed me to leave the tails of the turtles free in* Into the Deep End *(see page 73)*

Appliquéing your hearts

~ ❋ ~

Once you've prepared your four heart shapes,
one using each of the four methods,
it's time to do your first real piece of IMA!

1 Place your first prepared heart (the one with the freezer paper inside) on your background fabric and pin it in place. I honestly seldom pin because the pieces aren't too large, and with the freezer paper inside them they don't move around too much. Still, I respect the fact that many people feel more secure with pins, so 'Pin on, McDuff!' if you wish.

Take the appliqué pieces over to your sewing machine, which you should still have set up with the invisible thread on the top, the lightweight cotton in the bobbin, and the controls set for the blind hem stitch.

*In the following photographs I'm stitching with **BLACK** thread in place of the invisible nylon so that you can actually see what I am doing; of course your stitches, with the invisible thread, will be invisible!*

2 Begin stitching down one of the long, straight-ish sides of the heart. By the time you feel comfortable with the stitching you should be approaching the point; remember to keep counting your straight stitches, and make sure that you hold the fabric back so that you have a single bite at the point.

Now work your way up the other straight side of the heart (**a**), regain your composure and head for the first hump. When you're stitching round these, make use of your 'needle down' control, if you have one, or manually stop with the needle in the fabric so that it's easy to manoeuvre the fabric when necessary.

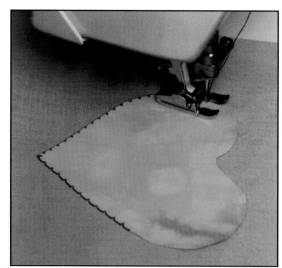

a

b

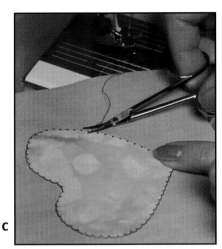

3 Now it's over the last hump and onto the final stretch (**b**), where you will meet up with your beginning stitches. Stitch over these, count for three straight stitches after a bite, back-stitch for two and stop. Now cut your threads (**c**) and admire your work.

Finally, before you stitch the appliquéd block into your quilt you must remove the freezer paper. Also, you must remove the paper before you stitch any secondary pieces that might go over your first piece. This is only scary the first time.

4 Use a small pair of sharp embroidery scissors and gently cut through the background fabric behind the appliquéd piece. You can feel the scissors hitting the freezer paper, and this provides you with some protection against cutting through to the appliqué fabric itself. Cut inside the appliquéd shape, leaving a scant ¼in seam allowance all round (**d**).

I know that some people go quite faint at the thought of cutting away the fabric from behind their appliqué. Let me assure you that I've been doing this for years, even when I don't have to remove freezer paper, without any ill effects. I feel that this technique allows the wadding to push slightly into the larger appliqué pieces and give them some dimension.

I don't feel that removing the background fabric in any way weakens the quilt. Once the quilt is finished the major stress is on the quilting stitches or the seams which hold the quilt together; if anything is going to give way, it will be these stitches, *not* the background. American Baltimore appliqué artist Ely Sienkiewicz agrees, as do many others. I feel that many of the well-known quilting 'no-no's' are more folklore than real good sense ...

5 Now, gently reach under the seam allowance and lift away the freezer paper (**e**). If the paper seems to be resisting, this simply means that your bites went a bit deeper into the appliqué piece and held onto the paper more: just get a firmer hold of it and tug (**f**). See, it's just like when you pulled out your first tooth: the really scary part is over, and you can be very proud that you did it!

Hooray for you! Isn't it lovely? What a team you and your machine make! Go on, give him a reassuring pat on the fly wheel; you both deserve praise.

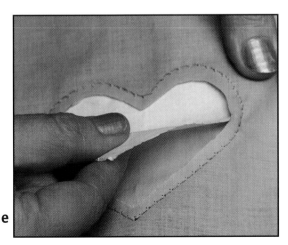

Other great ideas for using *the Invisible Stitch*

I constantly find additional ways to use this wonderful stitch. (You may discover more.) In this section I'd like to share a few of these ideas with you:

easy bias stems

appliquéing your appliqué! or 'Why cut borders?'

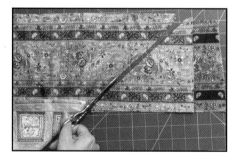

'Why curve piece when you can appliqué?'

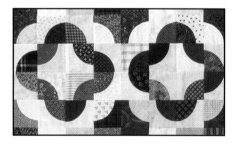

mitred borders

sewing on your labels

stained glass appliqué

Easy bias stems

~

Bias stems can come in many different sizes and shapes, and there are many very clever ways of making them. Here's a technique that I use regularly with great success for stems which curve in only one direction.

1 Use the 40° marking on your quilt rule and rotary-cut a strip no narrower than 1½in. Generally the original strip should be about 3 times the desired finished width of the stem, but I find that if I want a ¼in bias stem and I cut it ¾in wide, by the time I fold and press it there is very little left to hold on to. With a minimum strip of 1½inches I can cut away the excess fabric after it's stitched.

2 Fold the strip in half, wrong sides together, and press.

3 Position the stem on your background fabric and pin it in place. *NOTE: always lay the stem so that the **raw** edge is towards the **outside** of your curve. This way the folded edge will stretch to cover the raw edges. This is much easier than trying to coax the fold into the smaller inside of the curve.*

4 Sew a straight seam the distance *from the fold* that you want the finished stem to be (**a**).

5 Trim off any excess, then roll the folded edge over the seam to cover the stitching, as shown in steps **b** and **c**.

6 Check that your bias stems extend just beyond the ends of your stem line. Generally a stem is covered by a flower at one end, and the ground, a vase or something at the other end; if this isn't the case, allow a little extra and fold up the end of the stem before you roll the folded edge over the seam. This will give you a nicely finished end.

7 Re-set your machine for invisible machine appliqué, and IMA down the remaining side of the stem (**d**).

This technique can also be used if you're doing very traditional hand-work, as in Baltimore Album blocks. Sew your first securing seam on the machine, fold it over, and then stitch the remaining seam by hand. It will save you time, and no-one will ever know once the quilt is complete.

A variation of this technique, useful for stems which curve in both directions, is to use ready-prepared bias tape and IMA down both sides.

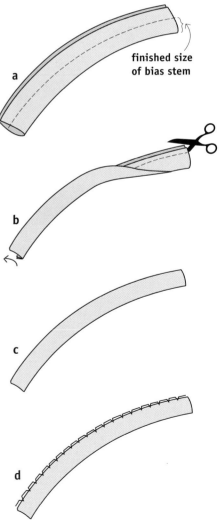

finished size of bias stem

a

b

c

d

Appliquéing your appliqué

~

S ometimes you're doing a small project and have a wonderful fabric for the borders. The only problem is that the fabric has large exciting designs on it. Or it has a very directional print. Or, as happened to me, it's a beautiful tartan/plaid ... except that the pattern is asymmetrical and therefore totally impossible to mitre.

So there I sat, staring at this yard of plaid that I desperately wanted around my fruit appliqué, totally mystified as to how to do it. Casually I laid my appliquéd piece down on the plaid and lamented on how beautiful it would have looked 'if only ...' Then it hit me – a bolt out of the blue – it was already done! I was looking so hard for a solution that the obvious answer completely missed me.

I spray-starched and ironed the plaid fabric. Then I lightly starched the appliqué piece and carefully pressed under $1/4$in seam allowance all the way around the piece. Placing the appliqué perfectly in the centre I pinned it and ran to my sewing machine to IMA it in place. It worked like a dream (below right). To this day no-one ever notices that the corners aren't really mitred; they just accept that they are. But if I had tried to cut, piece and mitre those borders in the traditional way I am sure everyone's eye would have been drawn to the odd match, and only after that would they have ever looked at the fruit ... and heck, that was the first fruit I ever drew, and although the shapes may not be the best ever, they are *my* fruit and I'm proud of them ...

For the quilt in the photo on the left I found a wonderful rabbit print which I wanted for my borders, but cutting it would have certainly resulted in decapitated rabbits and wasted fabric. So IMA came to the rescue again. Just be sure to measure carefully so that you get the blocks positioned exactly where you want them – and preferably straight.

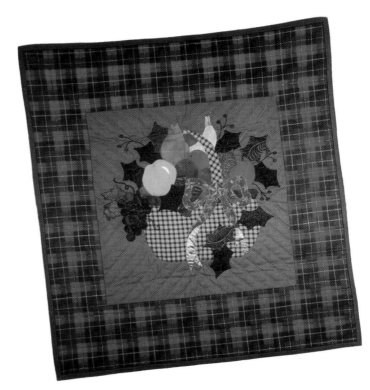

Appliquéd curves

~

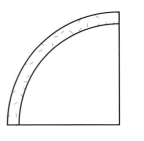

Why bother with fiddly curved piecing when you can appliqué the curves? I do terrible pieced curves. There: I've publicly admitted it – but I don't think that I'm alone. Whether I do them on the machine or by hand, my curves always look skew-whiffy. I get frustrated, then angry, then I look for someone to kick. By avoiding this technique altogether I had fewer grey hairs and my family fewer bruises, but I also had no curves!(*In my quilts,* that is!)

Wonderful blocks like the Drunkard's Path I avoided like the plague – until I realised that there was no rule set in stone that they had to be pieced. They simply had to be done and look good! Appliqué satisfies both of these criteria. Let me show you how...

1 Cut one 5in square of background fabric (**a**) and one 5in square of pattern fabric – or use the lower right-hand corner of your practice square.

2 Trace the full-size pattern (above right) onto the paper side of a bit of freezer paper and cut it out.

3 Place the printed fabric right side down on your ironing board, and place the freezer paper curve, waxy side down, on top of it. Match the straight edge of the freezer paper curve to the straight edge of the fabric square. Press.

4 Use Method 1; cut out, then spray-starch and press the edges of the fabric up and over the curved edge of the freezer paper (**b**).

5 Place the prepared curve onto the background square, matching the raw edges (**c**).

6 IMA the curved edge, cut away the background fabric and remove the freezer paper. (If you're careful this piece can be reused!)

Now wasn't that easy? A bit like eating popcorn – once you start you just can't stop.

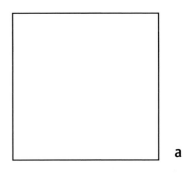

a

+

b

=

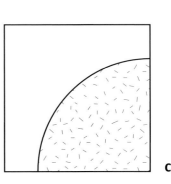

c

Mitred borders

~

a

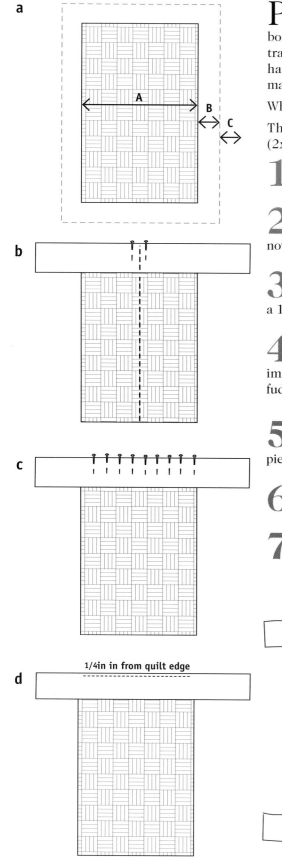

Printed borders, especially those created from specialised border-print fabric, make a stunning finish to any quilt. But matching those different borders can prove a real nightmare if you attempt to mitre your corners the traditional way (ie sewing a 45° angle from the reverse side). I have always hand-appliquéd my mitres *from the front*, so when I began doing invisible machine appliqué I saw no reason not to convert to doing my mitres with IMA.

When cutting your borders be sure to cut them:

The length of the centre of the quilt (A) + 2 x the width of *each* border (2xB); then add at least 6in extra (C) for good luck (see diagram **a**).

1 Mark the centre of this strip and find the centre of your quilt top. Pin the two together, right sides facing (**b**).

2 Pin to within ¼in of each edge (**c**). Attach the borders by machine, beginning and ending your stitching ¼in in from the quilt edge (**d**). You should now have long 'wings' of extra border fabric hanging off each end (**e**).

3 Once all four sides are attached, lay the quilt on an ironing board. Flatten out one end of the quilt and border, and press (**f**). Check with a 12 ½in square ruler to make sure that the edges are square (**g**).

4 Then lay the corresponding border strip over the first strip and fold at a 45° angle (**h**). Don't be too concerned about the angle, though, as the important thing is matching the designs and straight lines. If you have to fudge a bit to get everything to match, go right ahead!

5 Once everything matches to your satisfaction – and since you're working from the right side you can be sure that the match is correct – pin the pieces carefully and give the corner a good press (**i**).

6 Now take the quilt off to your machine to IMA in the usual way (**j**).

7 Turn the corner over and trim away the excess border fabric (**k**); you now have a perfectly mitred corner (**l**).

e   **f**

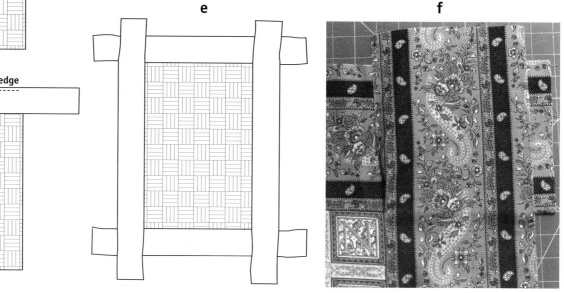

g

h

i

j

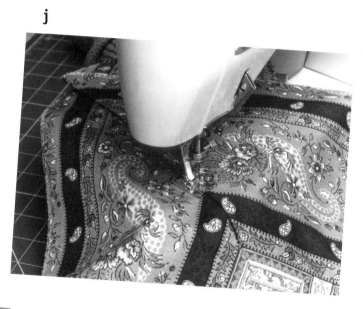

k

l

Attaching labels

~

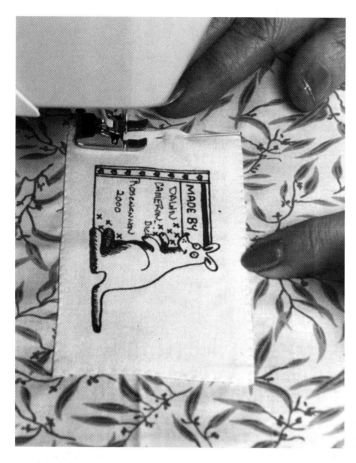

Your 'Made by...' label is an important part of your finished quilt. Unfortunately labels are often left to the last moment, given little thought or, worst of all, forgotten altogether. You may even dismiss the need for one as being boastful or too showy.

Poppycock!

Labels have nothing to do with vanity. You and your quilt are a team. You have been working together for a long time and it really doesn't deserve to be orphaned at this point.

Even those who do label often wait until the quilt is finished, then hastily sew on a scrap of calico onto which is scribbled some truly riveting information such as:

by ST Black '96

100 years from now, if the quilt survives, it will be an antique. Can't you just imagine some textile collector trying to work out whether this piece was made by

Shirley Temple Black in 1996
(thus creating a new twist on Hollywood history) or by

Silly Twit Black in 1896
(which would be a more appropriate assumption!)

Either way poor old Sarah Tessa Black who poured her heart and soul into it in 1996 will be totally forgotten. May I offer a few suggestions?

• **Invest in a good fabric pen.**

The Pigma Micron Pen is well tested as safe for fabrics. It doesn't 'feather' when the tip is placed on the fibres, and it will not make the fabric disintegrate over time. It's also light-resistant.

• **Look at some Dover publication books which are very often available at quilt fairs.**

These are copyright-free publications, so you may use their images with a clear conscience; they have a wonderful selection of borders, flowers and label designs.

• **You can use a light-box or window and trace these designs onto your fabric.**
You can also photocopy them and, if you press them within one hour with a hot dry iron, you can permanently transfer the design onto your fabric! It will be reversed, so this technique isn't good for any image that includes words.

• **But, better still, you can photocopy directly onto your fabric.**
Simply cut your fabric about 2in smaller on all sides than a piece of ordinary photocopying paper. Centre the pressed fabric on the paper and tape it down with Scotch Magic Tape (this is

the only tape I know of which won't melt in the copier). Now use a machine which has a hand feed tray on the side, and photocopy your information onto your fabric. After one hour press with a hot dry iron – it may be best to put a piece of paper between the image and your iron to prevent smears and/or a messy iron …

Shown on the right is a label I made for my quilt *Aunt Helen's Baskets*. I photocopied and reduced her engagement photo; then I printed out the text I wanted on my computer (you can also handwrite it if your penmanship is good), and put the two together on the photocopier to print directly onto my fabric.

I think it looks very nice, and it's certainly very personal!

Now that you have a pretty label, be sure to give us some interesting reading. How about:

Sarah Tessa Black
designed and made this quilt
for her daughter
Anna Black
on the occasion of her marriage to
Peter Moon
June 15, 2000
Glastonbury, Somerset, England

That should keep the quilt historians happy! Now you can sew it on, feeling very proud of yourself and your quilt.

But what if your great granddaughter has the scruples of a gnat and she carefully removes your label and replaces it with one of her own showing her as the creator? Paranoid? Maybe, but why take the chance. It has been done before.

Therefore I suggest attaching the label with invisible machine appliqué to the backing before you tack and quilt. Simply spray-starch the label, press under the edges and IMA it in the lower right-hand corner. Make sure that you position it a fair way up and into the body of the quilt so that you don't catch it in the binding.

This way your quilting will go through the label and your information will remain an integral part of YOUR quilt – as with the label below, which is on the back of *Chooks* (see page 61).

"AUNT HELENS BASKETS"
Made by Dawn Cameron-Dick
in memory of my
Aunt Helen Lewandowski
1907 - 1998

Stitched in spring 2000
at Rosenannon
East Sussex, UK

Stained glass appliqué

〜

There are many wonderful books on the this technique, such as Gail Lawther's *Stained Glass Patchwork* (also available from Teamwork Craftbooks), and many books of exciting patterns, so I won't attempt to duplicate that information here.

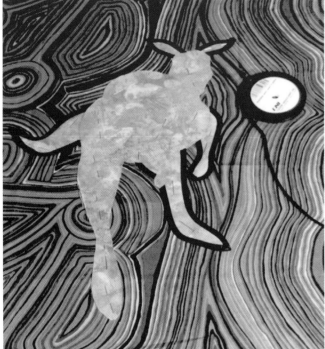

What I'd like you to think about is using invisible machine appliqué to stitch down those miles of bias tape, rather than stitching them by hand or top-stitching them by machine. The work will go twice as fast, and look just as good. Maybe better! Just remember always to stitch the inner curve first; then you can be sure that the outer one will behave.

Perhaps this is one place where you might try using the smoke-coloured nylon thread. As traditionally one uses mainly black bias binding, the darker thread may be just right. Of course if the majority of your appliqué fabrics are light-coloured it may show up more than you would like, but if you have bright or medium colours it could be perfect.

Choosing designs for IMA

TRADITIONAL...   OR...   CONTEMPORARY?

a

b

IT'S UP TO YOU!

Just about any design can be adapted to IMA, whether you want to start with a traditional design or create a modern look. In the flower block (**a**), even the pieced Flying Geese are appliquéd onto the background square as you can see from the back view (**c**). The free-form lily (**b**, and back view **d**) shows how unique or unusual fabrics can make a simple block exciting and modern.

reverse sides

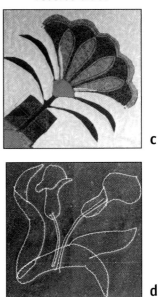

c

d

Most designs are suitable for invisible machine appliqué – and those which at first glance seem as though they aren't suitable can usually be made to work well by simplifying their shapes.

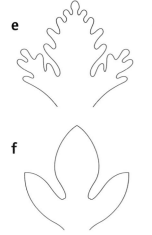

e

f

For example, the oak leaves in my quilt *Try To Remember...* (see the photo on the back cover) were too fiddly (**e**) for me to bother with the preparation necessary for IMA, so I happily did them by hand. But I could have chosen to eliminate some of the finer dips and created an oak leaf more like (**f**). And with an interesting choice of fabrics I think it would have been just as effective.

Look first for the design you really want to reproduce, and then see if you can adapt it to IMA. There's no point in choosing a design simply because it looks easier; always challenge yourself with something you really love. Then the process will be a labour of love and not just a means to an end.

If you can visualise it ... you can do it!

Where do designs come from?

~

Keep a camera or sketchpad with you so that you can record design ideas

L iterally everywhere. As a quilter I am sure you've already been teased for sketching the floor of the Louvre while everyone else is admiring the *Mona Lisa*. Or photographing the wallpaper in a public loo or the design of the seat fabric on a 747. The world abounds with ideas. The only difficult part is capturing them and adapting them to your needs.

• **Always keep a small camera handy**

Or at the very least, carry around a sketchpad and pencil. Try to retain the essence of the design, and let colour and perspective come later – you can always make quick written notes of particularly striking colour-schemes.

• **Source books**

Collins and Dover do extremely useful books with very clean and clear drawings which are copyright free. First, take the book to a photocopy machine which can enlarge, and have the image blown up to the size you want. Then take it home and lay some greaseproof paper over the design. With a pencil, trace the basic shapes (below). Leave out tiny details; you can add these later, or better still let your choice of fabrics suggest leaf veins, feathers or fur!

• Embroidery books

Books on different kinds of stitchery are another excellent source of ideas. Again you will want to enlarge and simplify, but the ideas are there. Just be sure, if you use someone else's idea, that you always give credit where credit is due. Designers have only their ideas to sell, and if you pinch them their kids eat stale bread and water.

• Quilt designs

Designs intended for quilting by hand or machine can often be adapted for appliqué. Just connect the lines, remove a few and you have a unique piece to appliqué.

• Nature

The natural world offers a wealth of ideas. Trace a leaf or a flower. Can't draw a garden fork? Photocopy it (or a suitable drawing or photograph) first, trace it and there you are!

• Children's books

These are a wonderful source, especially the colour books! My *Snow Sheep* (right) came from just such a book. These were actually hand appliquéd, but the shapes are perfect for IMA. Just trace the shapes onto freezer paper (if you're using method 1 they'll be reversed), cut your fabric pieces, and IMA them in numerical order.

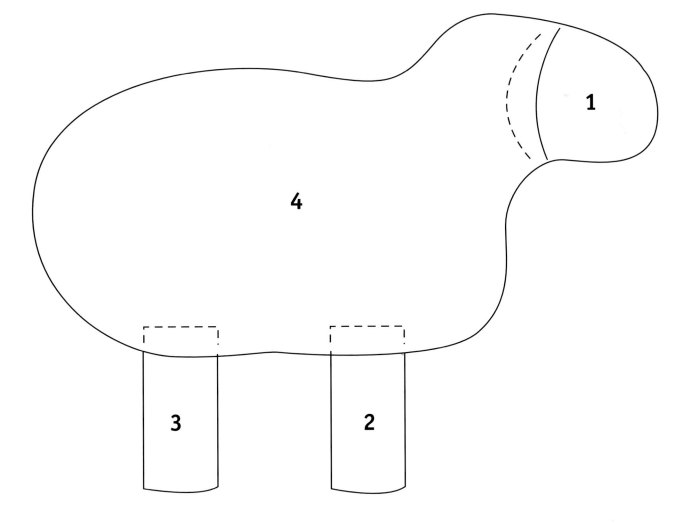

Stitching problems?

❈

Let me see if I can help.

Whenever things go wrong for me I always begin by:

- re-threading the machine
- brushing out any lint around the feed dogs and bobbin
- inserting a new needle

If this doesn't solve the problem I turn off the machine, have a cup of tea and take a pause to think ...

'My stitches are faulty'

If this is your problem, the cause could be:

- a defective needle (old, or poor-quality)
  if so, replace it with a new one
- the wrong size needle for your fabric
  use 60/9, 70/10 or 80/12 for most cottons
- the needle is in backwards, or not inserted completely
  the flat part should face the back of the machine, and the head of the needle should be all the way into the socket
- the pressure foot tension is too tight or too loose
  loosen or tighten it by adjusting the knob on the top of the machine (not all machines have these)
- you missed out a step while threading your machine
  re-thread the machine carefully, making sure that all the steps are in the correct order

'My tension is all wrong!'

Problems can often arise with the stitch or bobbin tension:

- different thread weights on the top and in the bobbin can cause problems
  match your threads whenever possible
- do you have threads stuck in the tension discs, or dirty discs?
  take your machine in for a service, or clean it with white spirit on a lint-free cloth
- threads wrapped round the bobbin case can create difficulties
  remove the bobbin case and clean it carefully
- do the problems with your stitch tension seem to be getting worse?
  has the machine been serviced recently? Take it in and have the timing re-set
- the bobbin thread shows on the top of the work
  tighten the bobbin screw slightly, or loosen the upper tension

Undoing IMA mistakes

Although I hate to bring it up, the moment does occasionally come when we have to admit ... we are not perfect. Yes, I know we've spent most of our lives trying to convince our kids, our parents and our partners that we are, but between you, me and the gatepost we can admit otherwise.

Sometimes it's not really a mistake, but an error of 'creative judgement,' or a sudden earthquake that pushes our appliqué piece out of line. Whatever the reason, you may one day wish to remove a piece you have attached by invisible machine appliqué.

Do not fret.....

I have found that the safest method is simply to lay the appliquéd block flat on a table, hold a seam ripper horizontal to the background fabric, and ever so gently encourage it along between the appliqué piece and the background. The curved blade will nip away at the bites, and in no time your appliqué piece will be free.

The remaining threads will be easy to remove if you flip over to the back and pull on the bobbin thread. As the bites have been cut, the bobbin thread just unravels and all you have to do is brush away the remaining invisible thread.

If you've discovered the error before you've removed the freezer paper, you haven't destroyed the appliqué piece and it's ready to be re-appliquéd. Easy.

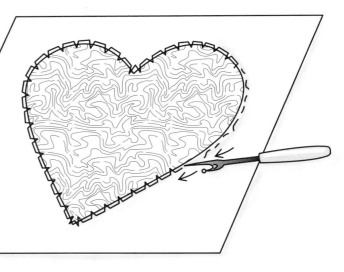

If it happens after the freezer paper has been removed, still follow the same course (perhaps a wee bit more carefully, to ensure that you don't pull the background out of shape) and then re-make the offending appliqué piece.

As a final thought ... learn to love your 'mistakes'; they could end up making your quilt just that little bit more special!

REMEMBER ... We do this for fun.

It's a leisure-time recreation. If a project ever stops being enjoyable and becomes a chore, it may be best to set it aside for a while and re-evaluate. A solution may come to you in the night, or perhaps it will just look better at a later date.

As Scarlett says, 'Tomorrow is another day!' Granted she was no scholar, but it sure makes sense to me ...

General instructions for the projects

~ �֍ ~

Ignore these at your own peril!

Preparation

~

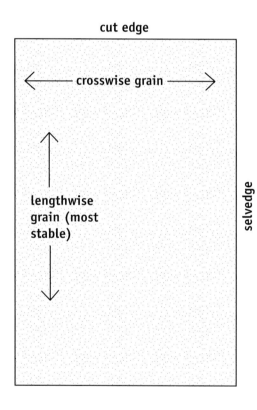

cut edge

← **crosswise grain** →

↑
lengthwise grain (most stable)
↓

selvedge

- All designs are suitable for either hand appliqué or invisible machine appliqué.

- Wash and press all fabrics before use.

- Generously spray-starch all fabrics that will be rotary cut, to give them extra stability.

- I've written all the fabric requirements assuming that your fabric has a width of 40 useable inches (102cm). Always cut selvedge to selvedge unless the instructions specify otherwise (eg some of the instructions I've given for borders require using the lengthwise grain for stability, and thus you don't need to piece them).

- Mark on your fabrics only with a pre-tested pencil or fabric pen.

- All seam allowances are designed for a scant ¼in; constantly check your seam allowances as you stitch.

- Make any necessary templates with plastic mylar or cardboard. All the templates for the patterns I've included are drawn finished size; you don't need to add seam allowances to the templates themselves.

Pressing

~

This is one of the most important factors in a well-made quilt. Press your work after each seam you sew. I don't ever use a steam iron as I feel that it distorts the fabric. Press from the back if you're worried about melting the nylon thread – it won't melt, but you might worry that it will! Press all seams to the darker fabric; I don't recommend pressing your seams open except in the most unusual circumstances, and I'll mention these clearly in the text.

Backing fabric

I don't usually include specific fabric requirements for backing your quilt. Today there are so many widths of suitable fabric available that it would be difficult to be accurate – but again, do be creative in your choices.

If you need to piece the backing, try not to put a seam directly down the middle. Over time this tends to show on the front as a small ridge. It may be better to split one length of fabric and put one strip on each side of your full-width piece, as shown below. I *do* press these seams open, incidentally.

Think about adding a design to the back as well. On my *Chooks* quilt my mother suggested adding a friend for the ladies on the front. The simple rooster (shown right) always makes people smile in surprise, and definitely made for a better quilt. After all, the reverse side of a quilt is seen almost as much as the front, especially in the case of a child's comforter or a lap quilt.

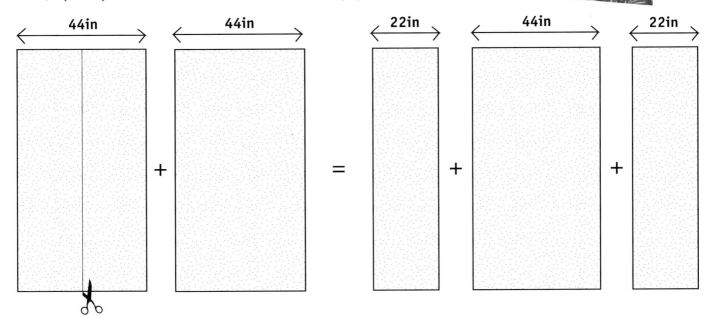

A word on waddings

Your choice of wadding is another very personal matter. Over the past 20 years 90% of my hand-quilted quilts have been made using a low loft, 2oz polyester wadding made by Mountain Mist called *Quilt Lite*. It's available in the USA and on the continent, but as far as I know it's not available in the UK. The Hobbs company makes a lovely one called *Polydown*, which needles very well and which I have used successfully. And, of course, there is wool, which is expensive but exquisite!

For machine quilting a 100% cotton or an 80/20 cotton/polyester blend is nice and easy to work with. Try to avoid ones that need pre-washing. Hobbs makes a nice one called *Heirloom Cotton*, and Fairfield makes one called *Soft Touch*; I've used both with good results.

I always use waddings that are made to the size I require. I look upon the task of piecing wadding with about the same attitude that I have to making my own mayonnaise – why bother? It's never as good! Always be sure that your wadding is distinctly larger than your quilt top; as you stitch the wadding may pull in, and you will almost certainly end up with some of your border being unpadded. Again, this advice comes from hard-learned experience.

One last word on wadding ... try to find a brand you like and stick to it. Experiment on a small square before you commit yourself to using it in your quilt: once you've tacked, you're very unlikely to untack and replace the wadding if you find that quilting it is as much fun as swimming through quicksand (hearsay only ... rest assured that I haven't made that mistake!) Keep a note of waddings you like and which ones you used on which quilt for future reference. Quilters always appreciate recommendations on waddings!

Quilting

As this is a book about invisible machine appliqué I've decided not to include quilting patterns or instructions. They take up too much space which I'd rather devote to the appliqué itself; and besides, I feel that quilting is a personal choice which makes your work uniquely your own. So be creative.

As a basic guideline, for hand quilting I use only neutral-coloured cotton thread (YLI or JP Coats are my favourites), and I don't generally use more than *one colour per quilt*.

For machine quilting I use either YLI Wonder Invisible thread, or a light-weight cotton to match the fabric I'm quilting. Often I straight-line quilt by machine in the ditch around each block, then go back and do my hand quilting in the open areas that really show!

Bindings

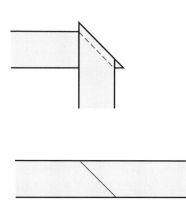

I always make a separate, double-folded binding. I cut my strips six times the width of the finished binding (eg $^1\!/_2$in finished = cut 3in wide). I cut them selvedge to selvedge, and then piece them together end to end with an angled seam as shown on the left; again, I do press this seam open to reduce the bulk when the strip is folded. Then I press the strips in half, wrong sides together; I sew them on with my walking foot, and they look great. Before you begin adding the border, use a large cutting mat, long ruler and a square rule to trim all edges of your quilt sandwich so that they are even and at right angles.

I seldom make bias binding. I find it wasteful of fabric and a bear to handle, and today even my 25-year-old, well-used quilts have stable, intact bindings. If you prefer to use bias-cut bindings, though, that's fine; it's totally up to you.

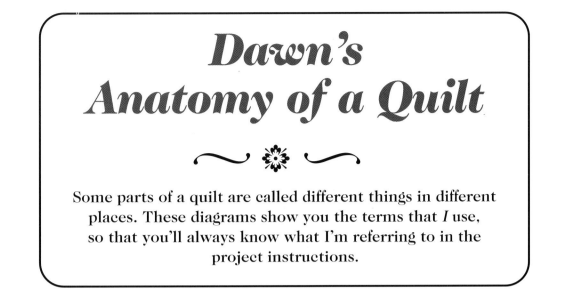

Dawn's Anatomy of a Quilt

Some parts of a quilt are called different things in different places. These diagrams show you the terms that *I* use, so that you'll always know what I'm referring to in the project instructions.

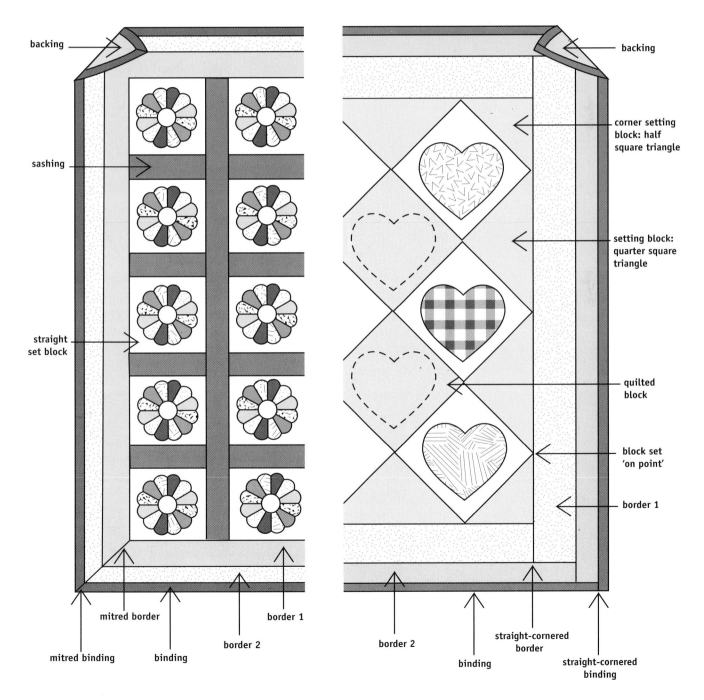

backing

sashing

straight set block

mitred border

mitred binding

binding

border 2

border 1

backing

corner setting block: half square triangle

setting block: quarter square triangle

quilted block

block set 'on point'

border 1

straight-cornered border

straight-cornered binding

border 2

binding

Keukenhof (Tulips)

Size: 74in (188cm) square; four 19in (48cm) blocks

~

SKILL LEVEL: *intermediate*

TECHNIQUES REQUIRED:
*basic rotary cutting skills for pieced borders;
method 1 or 2 (see pages 24 & 27);
method 4 (see page 30)
bias stems*

~

I designed Keukenhof *after teaching at Quilt Expo III in the Netherlands, when the tulip fields were in full bloom. The simplicity and power of the elegant tulip, swaying on its lofty stem, challenged me to use some of the lovely hand-dyed fabrics I'd been collecting. I kept it a simple four-block quilt framed with a brightly-pieced inner border and a tiny 'pleat' of colour at the edges. This left me with wonderful open spaces where I hand-quilted bunches of tulips and feathered swags!*

MATERIALS:
- Assorted solids and hand-dyed-look pastels for the tulips, to total about 1yd (4in squares of each fabric are ideal)
- 5yd (4.5m) white background fabric
- 1¼yd (115cm) purple 'accent' fabric
- ½yd (50cm) bright green for the stems
- ½yd (50cm) 'mottled' or marbled green for the leaves
- Fabric pencil

CREATING THE BLOCKS

1 From the white background fabric cut out four 20in (50.5cm) squares for the background blocks.

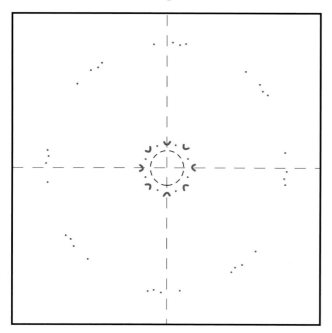

2 Fold each square into quarters to find the centre. Then use the placement guide on page 56 and a fabric pencil to mark the base of each leaf and tulip stem, as shown left. (I use faint dots and dotted lines.)

3 From the stem fabric, cut 1in (2.5cm)-width bias strips for stems. You will need about 5in (13cm) length per tulip, and a total length of about 40in (102cm) per block.

4 Prepare the leaves and tulip petals using your favourite method: I used method 1 (see page 24) for mine. I thought that a bright solid for the background petals with a hand-dyed centre petal looked good.

5 The circles at the centre of each block are 1¾in (4.5cm) diameter when finished. Prepare these using method 4; circles lie best this way.

6 Appliqué the stems first, using the 'easy bias stems' method on page 35. Use IMA to appliqué the leaves, and to add the tulip flowers to cover the tops of the stems. Finish off with the centre circles, over the lower ends of the stems. Trim and square up the block to measure 19½ in (49.5cm).

PIECING THE ACCENT BORDER AND ADDING THE SETTING TRIANGLES

1 Cut twelve 2in (5cm) strips (selvedge to selvedge) of background fabric, and six 2in (5cm) strips of your accent colour.

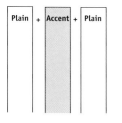

2 Join the strips as shown (far left); press towards the dark fabric, and sub-cut into 2in (5cm) units.

3 Sew the units together, offsetting each unit as shown, then trim away the zigzag edges along the lines shown below: make sure that you leave a ¼ in (5mm) seam allowance beyond the tips of the accent colour squares.

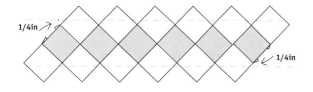

4 Sew the strips onto the blocks in the order shown below.

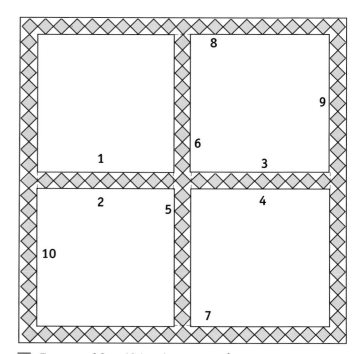

5 Cut two 33in (84cm) squares for the background, and cut each of them diagonally into two half-square triangles as shown below. Handle the pieces carefully as they have very long bias edges!

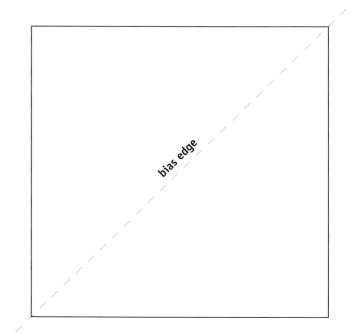

6 Stitch the triangles onto the edges of the central pieced square; work with the bias edge of the background fabric against your machine's feed dogs to minimise stretching.

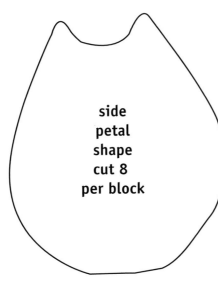

side
petal
shape
cut 8
per block

centre petal
cut 8
per block

leaf
cut 8
per block

centre circle,
1³/₄in finished;
cut 2 per block
and make up using
method 4

ADDING THE ACCENT PLEAT AND OUTER BORDER

1 Cut eight 1¹/₂in (4cm) strips of accent fabric; stitch together end to end. Press these in half, wrong sides together; this will create your pleat.

2 Cut eight 6in (15cm) outer borders from the background fabric. Sew these together in pairs to form four strips 6in (15cm) wide and 80in (204cm) long; press centre seam open.

3 Lay prepared folded accent strips along the inner edges of the border strips and sew in place as shown below.

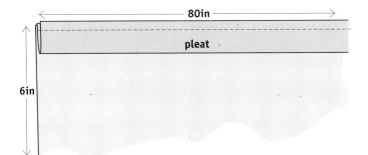

4 Lay one border strip down the side of the pieced unit, right sides together, so that the seam of border strip is at the centre of the outermost accent square: pin in place.

5 Begin sewing the border ¹/₄in (5mm) from the edge of the pieced block and stop ¹/₄in from the other edge. Add the other border pieces in the same way.

6 Follow the instructions on page 38 to mitre and IMA the border.

FINISHING

1 Add the wadding and backing in the usual way, and quilt the prepared top by hand or machine. I quilted bunches of tulips in each corner setting block and then echoed the gridded design of the accent border. When the quilting is complete, bind the quilt in your chosen fabric; I used the same colour I chose for the accent squares and the pleat.

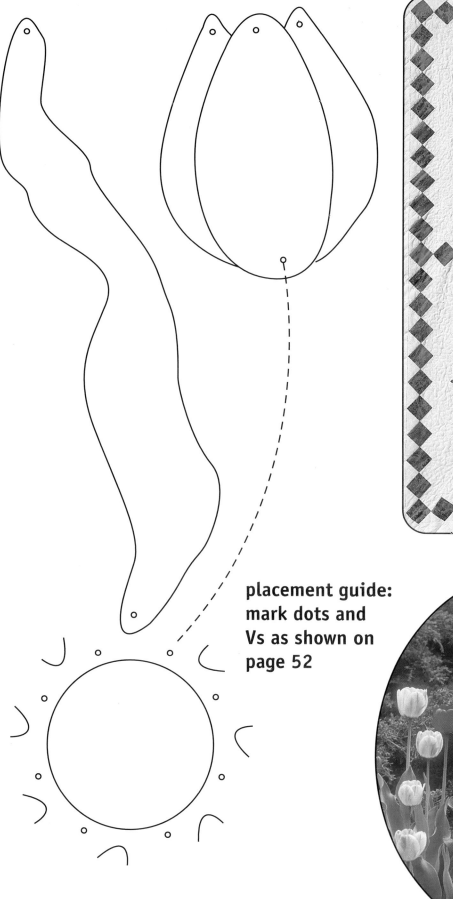

placement guide:
mark dots and
Vs as shown on
page 52

Country Hearts

Size: 36in (92cm) square; four 8½in (21.5cm) blocks

SKILL LEVEL: *suitable for all levels*

TECHNIQUES REQUIRED:
*method 2, freezer paper shiny side up (see page 27);
mitred borders (see page 38)*

*By chance I found this lovely yellow striped fabric very cheaply in a
discount fabric shop near my home in Waterloo, Belgium. It was a
border calling out for a quilt! I kept the hearts simple so that the
piece wouldn't be overpowered by colour. Make more hearts, use up
scraps and make a full-size quilt – or wouldn't it be cute for a baby?*

MATERIALS:

- Sixteen 5in (13cm) squares of fabric that co-ordinate in sets of four. Go for variety in prints, plaids, stripes, large and small flowers!·
- $1/4$ yd (20cm) or fat quarter background fabric 1 (pale)
- $1/4$ yd (20cm) or fat quarter background fabric 2 (dark)
- $1^1/4$ yd (115cm) border fabric: I used a printed stripe, you could piece one instead!
- $1/8$ yd (15cm) contrast fabric for sashing
- $1/2$ yd (45cm) binding fabric

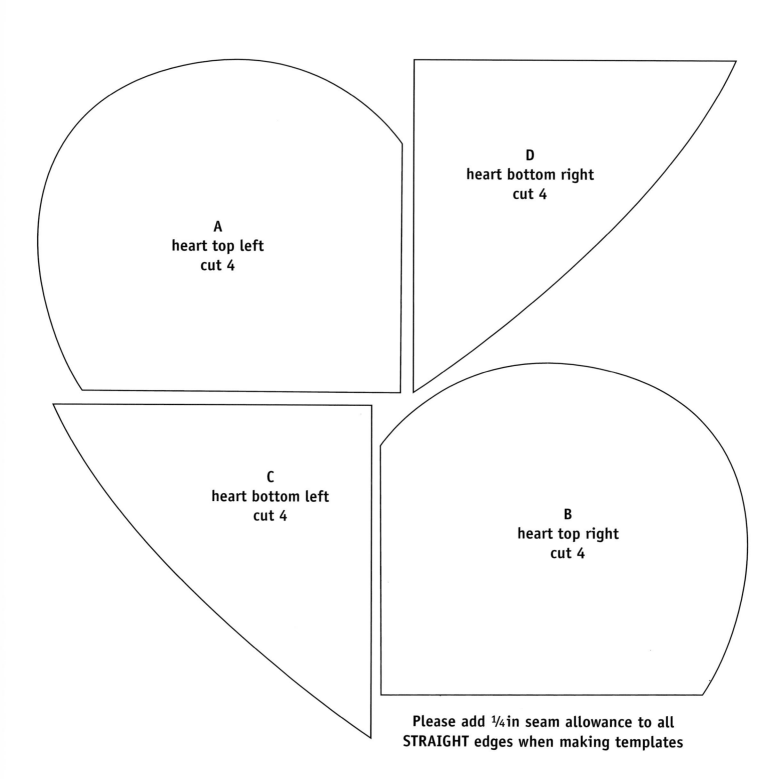

**A
heart top left
cut 4**

**D
heart bottom right
cut 4**

**C
heart bottom left
cut 4**

**B
heart top right
cut 4**

Please add $1/4$ in seam allowance to all STRAIGHT edges when making templates

CREATING THE HEART BLOCKS

1 Cut sixteen 4³/4in (11cm) background squares from your dark and pale background fabrics; I used eight dark and eight pale.

2 Trace templates A-D (opposite). Use these shapes as templates for cutting the following shapes from freezer paper:

- four left-hand heart tops (template A)
- four right-hand heart tops (template B)
- four left-hand heart bottoms (template C)
- four right-hand heart tops (template D)

3 The sixteen small squares of fabric are used for the different sections of the heart shapes; there are four hearts, which each use one set of four fabrics. 'Audition' each set of fabrics to find the most pleasing position for each individual fabric on the heart. When you've decided, use the cut freezer paper shapes to prepare all the heart sections for appliqué. Use your favourite freezer paper method: I used method 2.

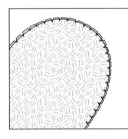

4 Appliqué the heart sections to the background squares. Only appliqué curved edges; the straight edges will line up with the raw edges of the background blocks and be sewn in the seams.

5 Sew each set of four appliquéd background blocks into squares; join the two top sections of the heart together first, then the two bottom sections. Finally, join the tops to the bottoms. You now have four complete heart blocks.

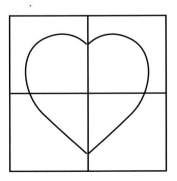

CONSTRUCTING THE QUILT

1 Decide on the layout of your blocks: I used a block with the dark background at the top left and bottom right, and a block with the pale background top right and bottom left. Cut two strips of sashing fabric 1¹/2x9in (4x23cm), and sew one between each pair of heart blocks.

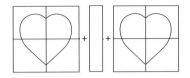

2 Cut one 1¹/2x 18¹/2in (4x47cm) strip of sashing and sew it between these two units; set this section aside.

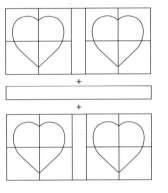

3 Cut four strips from the border fabric, each 16x40in (41x102cm).

4 Cut four strips from the sashing fabric, each 1¹/2x22in (4x56cm): sew these onto the inner edges of the border strips, matching the centres of the strips.

5 Stitch one combined border/sashing unit onto each edge of the quilt. Mitre the corners and IMA them.

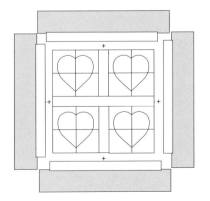

6 Quilt the design as you wish, then bind the edges with 3¹/2in (9cm) strips of binding fabric cut on the straight grain of the fabric.

Chooks

Size: 52x70in (132x180cm); twelve 11½in (29cm) blocks (cut 12in, 30cm), plus 8in (20cm) strip-pieced border (including 'cheat strips')

SKILL LEVEL: *beginner*

TECHNIQUES REQUIRED:
method 1, freezer paper and spray starch (see page 24);
chain stitch embroidery for the legs, French knots for the eyes

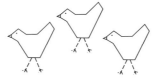

Chooks (Australian slang for chickens) was named by our 'adopted' Aussie daughter Julie Mountain, who regularly tries to secrete it in her back-pack whenever she leaves us on her travels.

My ever-growing collection of plaids was crying out to be used, and we needed a sofa quilt. Chickens seemed a fine choice. The sharp lines, easy points and lack of curves make this a perfect choice for beginning IMA. If the pieced border is too intimidating, feel free to replace it with a favourite plaid or maybe some appropriate barnyard print fabric. Either way, I am sure these chooks will always make you smile.

MATERIALS:
- 12in (30cm) squares of twelve different background fabrics (or three or four different fabrics to total 1½yd/1.5m)
- 9in (23cm) squares of twelve different chicken fabrics (or three or four different fabrics to total 1yd/1m)
- 6in (15cm) squares of six different baby chicken fabrics (or three or four different fabrics to total ¼yd/25cm)
- Assorted light plaids or stripes for the pieced border, totalling ⅝yd (60cm)
- Assorted dark plaids or stripes for the border, totalling 1yd (1m)
- 35x10in (89x25cm) strip of 'grass' or 'straw' fabric for the babies to scratch around on
- 6in (15cm) square of double-sided bonding web
- ¾yd (70cm) binding fabric
- Scraps of red and yellow fabric for beaks, combs and nests
- Six-strand embroidery thread in yellow and black

MAKING THE BLOCKS

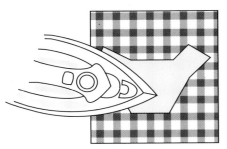

1 Trace the body of the large chicken twelve times onto the paper side of your freezer paper. Cut out all these shapes and press one onto the wrong side of each square of chicken fabric.

2 Following method 1 (see page 24), paint the area around each chicken with spray starch.

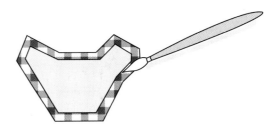

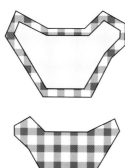

3 Cut out all the chicken shapes, allowing a generous 1/4in seam allowance.

4 Use a hot, dry iron to press the seam allowance over the freezer paper. Press until the seam is dry and it will form a crisp, clean edge for you to appliqué.

5 Choose a background fabric for each chicken. On each square, position the chicken on the right side of the background fabric, with the 'X' at the centre of the square, and pin.

6 Draw the beak and comb shapes twelve times onto the paper side of the bonding web square. Cut round each shape roughly. Lay the cut shapes, web side down, on the wrong sides of the scraps of red and yellow fabric and press them.

7 Cut the shapes out along the drawn lines and remove the pieces of backing paper. Place these pieces in the correct position behind the chickens' heads. Remove the chicken bodies and iron the beaks and combs in place. (I then top-stitched the beaks and combs in place by machine, using a very short stitch, for security and emphasis.)

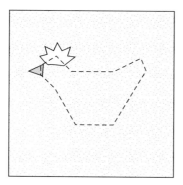

8 Replace the chicken bodies and IMA them in position, making sure that the straight stitches fall on the background and only the 'bites' bite the chicken!

9 Cut away the background fabric behind the body and remove the freezer paper.

10 Stitch legs onto nine of the chickens; the legs should be about 3in (7cm) long. The appeal of these chickens comes from their quirkiness; stitch some legs straight and some pairs at angles (see the main photograph). I embroidered the legs using two strands of yellow thread and chain stitch: I then added a French knot eye with two strands of black wrapped three times around the needle.

THE NESTS AND THE BABY CHICKS PANEL

1 Cut two 6x2in (15x5cm) pieces of yellow print fabric. Place the strips wrong sides together, and stitch down the centre with a long straight stitch (by hand or machine) to hold the strips together.

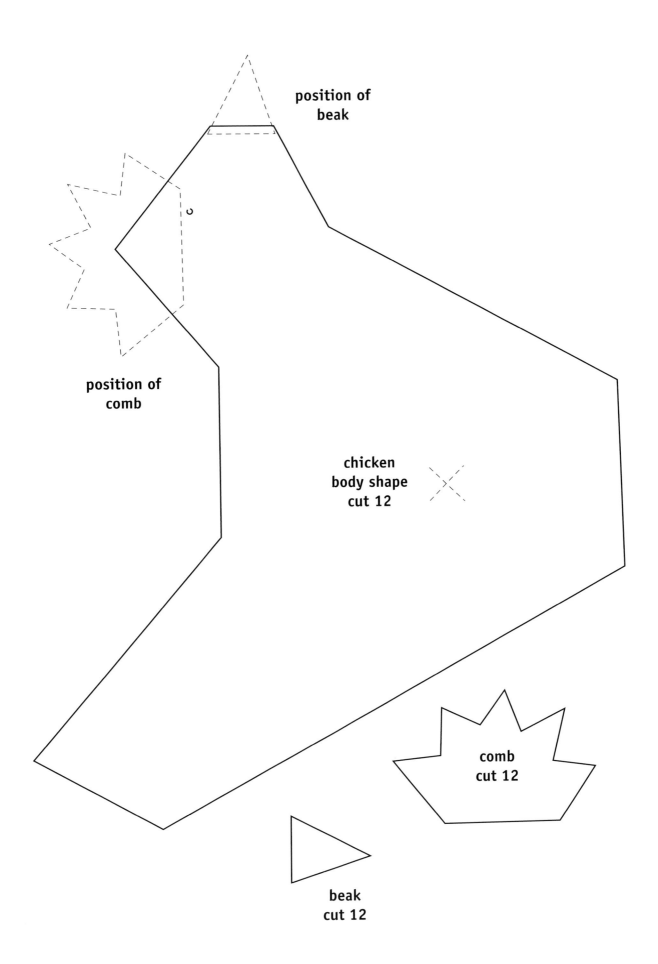

position of
beak

position of
comb

chicken
body shape
cut 12

comb
cut 12

beak
cut 12

2 Fold the fabric on the stitched line, then clip the fabric every ¹/₄in (5mm) or so, stopping well short of the holding stitch.

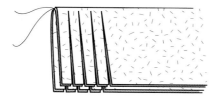

3 Knot the thread at one end of the line of stitching, and pull on the other end until the strip begins to gather. Pull it up to about 3¹/₂in (9cm), and securely tie the threads off. Create three nests in this way and appliqué a gathered nest under each remaining chicken shape.

4 Using the template at the bottom of this page, prepare and appliqué six baby chicks in assorted positions along your strip of grass or straw fabric. Follow the instructions for the large chickens; the only difference is that the babies have no head-gear! Also, for a bit of fun I cut out one of the babies facing the other way, and stitched him on at an angle – I'm sure every coop has its non-conformist ...

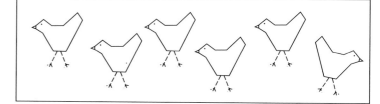

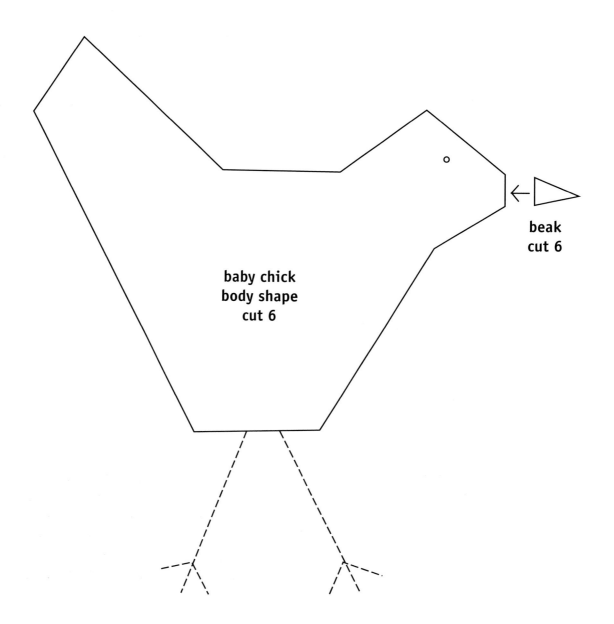

**beak
cut 6**

**baby chick
body shape
cut 6**

PIECING THE CENTRAL PANEL

1 Lay the chicken squares out and find the most pleasing arrangement of the background patches. I put all the 'nesting' chickens on the bottom row, but you could dot them around if you prefer. Once you're happy with the arrangement, join the chicken blocks in rows of three.

2 Join the four rows of three, then add the baby chicks panel to the bottom of the pieced section to create the central unit (right).

PIECING THE BORDER

1 From your assorted plaids and strips for the border, cut 6in (15cm) squares: nineteen dark and twenty-one light.

2 Make two diagonal cuts across each square to create four quarter-square triangles (right).

CAUTION: quarter-square triangles have two bias edges! Handle the edges with care so that they don't stretch.

3 Piece one light triangle to one dark triangle, right sides together, and continue doing this to make strips of triangles (below).

4 Then join two strips, light triangles to light triangles, offsetting the light patches to create a zigzag effect (below). On the border there are 17 light patches across the top and 25 down each side, as shown in the diagram on page 66.

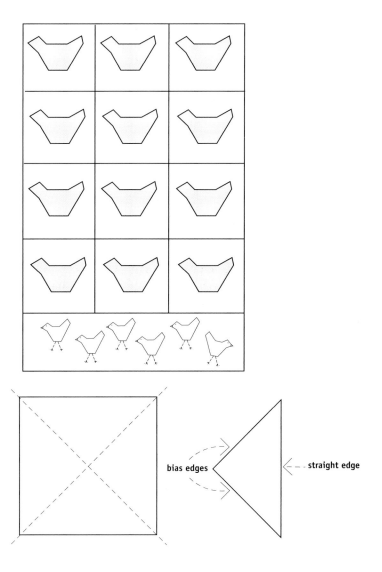

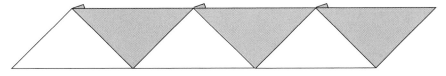

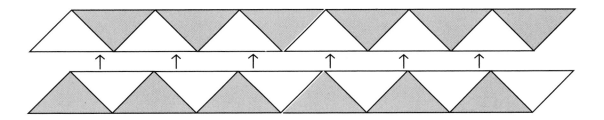

5 Once the borders are pieced (**e**), lay them out with the appliquéd and pieced central panel. Cut and sew 'cheater' strips (**f**) to fill in the space between the two (remember to add ½in/1cm to the length and width of each strip for seam allowances). The width required for the top and sides may be different – it certainly was on mine – so **don't** attempt to mitre them: just use a straight setting.

FINISHING AND BINDING

1 From your leftover dark fabrics, cut about twenty-four 3x12in (7.5x30cm) rectangles to make a final border. Sew the rectangles end to end, then use these to create an outer band beyond the zigzag border (**g**).

2 Add the wadding and backing fabric, and quilt as you wish. I outlined the chickens, and then did a cross-hatching pattern across the background with black quilting thread.

3 From your binding fabric, cut eight 3in (7.5cm)-wide strips on the straight grain. Sew these end to end in pairs, wrong sides together, to create four long strips, pressing the joining seams open. Use these strips to bind the edges of your quilt.

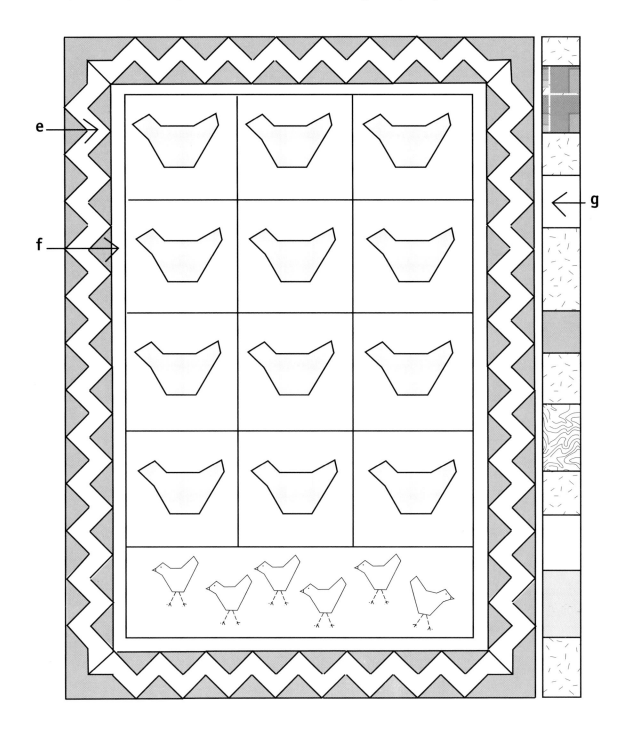

This is the rooster design I used on the back of my own Chooks quilt. If you want to do the same, enlarge Mr Rooster to 18in (46cm) high, and IMA him in the centre of your backing fabric before you make your quilt sandwich. I used leaf, rock and geometric prints to make my rooster look real.

I made his comb three-dimensional, using Method 4 (see page 30); his claws were fabric-bonded and top-stitched in the same way as the chickens' beaks and combs.

Album Rose

Size: *30in (76cm) square; four 12in (30cm) blocks,*

SKILL LEVEL: *confident beginner*

TECHNIQUES REQUIRED:
*method 1, freezer paper and spray starch (see page 24);
no special skills involved*

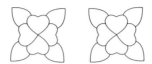

*I think the heart is a very useful shape; I use it often to teach both
hand and machine appliqué. It seems to have it all – straight lines,
gentle curves, a dip and a nice point. So I wanted a design that
would utilise this wonderful shape but in a slightly different way.
This 'rose' is actually four individual hearts touching at their
points. The addition of four simple leaves and a puff centre creates
an almost Tudor-like rose design. I've set them in a frame with
curved edges to mimic the look of an old photo album, where photos
are attached with those lovely black corners!*

MATERIALS:
- ⁊/8yd (80cm) background fabric
- Hearts and puffs 1/2yd (50cm)
- Leaves 1/4yd (25cm) (or fat quarter)
- 3/4yd (70cm) contrast fabric for the sashing, borders and binding

MAKING THE FLOWERS

1 Cut four 12¹/2in (31.5cm) squares from your background fabric. Fold each square in half diagonally, then in half again; press the folds.

2 Trace or photocopy template A on page 71, and use this to prepare sixteen leaf shapes using your favourite method (I used method 1). Now trace template B, and use this to prepare sixteen heart shapes in the same way.

3 Position four leaves onto each block of background fabric so that their bases are 2in (5cm) away from the centre point and their tips align with the diagonal folds; IMA the leaves, and cut away the back to remove the freezer paper (see page 33).

4 On one block, position the first heart to create the first petal of the rose (a), and begin to appliqué at the dot marked; continue around to the point. Cut away the back and remove the freezer paper.

5 Working clockwise round the flower, position the second heart, which will slightly overlap the first one (b); IMA round the entire edge. Repeat with the remaining hearts (c) to create the complete rose; the final heart will tuck underneath the first one, and you can then IMA the remaining edge of the first heart. Repeat this process with the remaining three blocks.

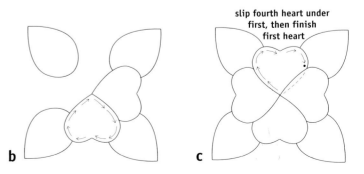

slip fourth heart under first, then finish first heart

a   b   c

SUFFOLK PUFF OR
YOYO CENTRES

1 Cut four 3in (7.5cm) circles from the hearts fabric. Thread a hand-sewing needle with extra-strong thread; use a double strand and knot the end.

2 With the wrong side of the circle facing upwards, begin turning a 1/8-1/4in (3-5mm) seam allowance to the wrong side. Hide the knot by inserting the needle into the fold. Turn the seam allowance down as you make a row of running stitches very close to the folded edge. These stitches shouldn't be too small; the larger the yoyo, the larger the stitches will need to be in order to pull the centre up tightly.

3 Continue folding the seam allowance and stitching around the circle until you reach the beginning. Pull up the stitches tightly to close the centre of the circle. Smooth and flatten the circle with your fingertips; the hole should be in the exact centre. The side with the hole is usually considered the front or right side.

4 Take a couple of small stitches and knot the thread to secure it. (You can also run the thread through to the back of the yoyo.) If the centre opening looks too big, try making larger stitches on your next circle. Slipstitch a yoyo into the centre of each flower shape (**d**).

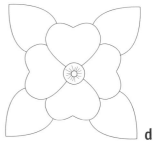

d

CREATING THE FRAME

1 Trace or photocopy template C and use it to prepare sixteen 'corner' shapes from freezer paper and your border fabric.

2 Position one 'corner' in the corner of each flower block; IMA the curved edge only (the straight edges will be hidden in the seams of the blocks), and press (e).

e

STITCHING THE SASHING AND BORDER

1 From your border fabric, cut:

- two strips 1½x12in (4x30cm); these are strips D.
- three strips 1½x25½in (4x64cm); these are strips E.
- two strips 1½x27½in (4x70cm); these are strips F.

2 Sew one strip D between each pair of flower blocks (below). Sew one strip E to join the two flower units, and one on each side of the unit (above right). Sew the F strips to the top and bottom of the pieced unit (centre right). Press seams to the sashing.

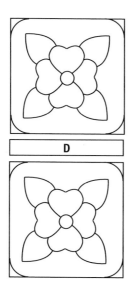

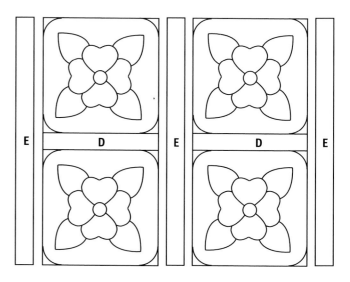

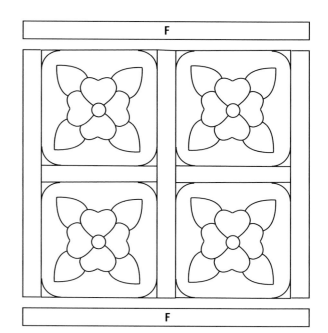

3 From the background fabric, cut:

- two strips 1x27½in (2.5x70cm); these are strips G.
- two strips 1x28½in (2.5x72.5cm); these are strips H.

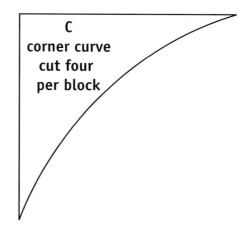

C
corner curve
cut four
per block

4 Sew strips G and H to the edges of the pieced unit to create the first border, as shown below.

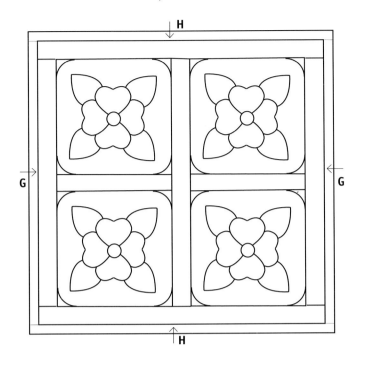

5 From the border fabric, cut:

- two strips $1\frac{1}{2}$ x$28\frac{1}{2}$in (4x72.5cm); these are strips I.
- two strips $1\frac{1}{2}$x$30\frac{1}{2}$in (4x77.5cm); these are strips J.

6 Sew strips I and J to the edges of the pieced unit to create an outer border, as shown below.

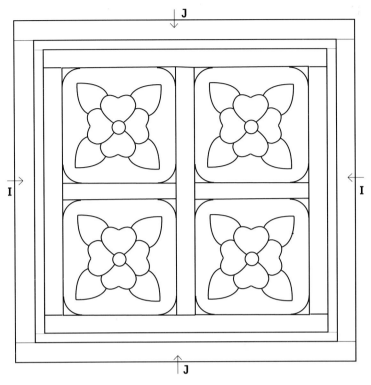

FINISHING

1 Add the wadding and backing fabric, then quilt the design as you wish; I quilted the rose designs 'in the ditch,' then added some straight lines radiating out from the flower centres.

2 Cut four 3x40in (7.5x102cm) strips from your border fabric, and use these to bind the quilt.

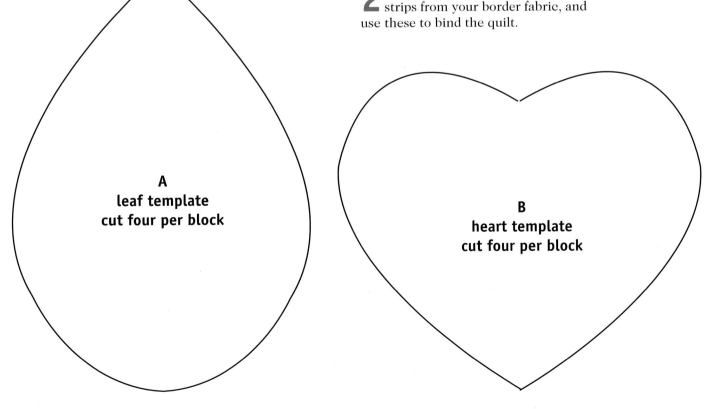

A
leaf template
cut four per block

B
heart template
cut four per block

Into the Deep End

Size: 44x66in (112x168cm); eight 10in (25cm) turtle blocks,
7¹/₂in (19cm) cut borders

SKILL LEVEL: *easy*

TECHNIQUES REQUIRED:
method 1, freezer paper and spray starch (see page 24);
method 4, lining with fabric (see page 30)
no special skills required

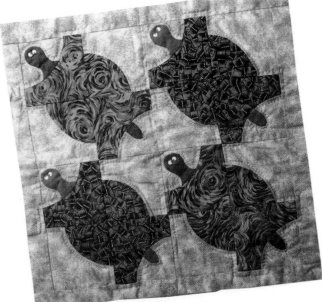

Into The Deep End *grew from my fascination with the Drunkards Path block. I first made this turtle design smaller, as a cushion called* Sand Turtles *(see photo below), with the fabrics being chosen by my son Alastair. This time I added 3D tails and enlarged the blocks to make a child's quilt. A lucky fabric find at Quilts UK 99 resulted in good-sized pebbles for the shore, and a lovely waterlike blue; I used both sides of the blue to represent the deeper and shallower water (hence the name).*

I have glued on 'googly' eyes as they make me laugh, but if you're actually going to be making this for a child I would strongly recommend that you embroider the eyes. Or try sewing on some buttons securely!

MATERIALS:
- 1¹/₂yd (1.5m) rock or sand fabric
- 1¹/₄yd (115cm) water fabric
- ¹/₂yd (45cm) dark/mottled green for the turtle shells
- ¹/₄yd (20cm) for heads and tails
- stranded embroidery cotton for the eyes (or buttons, or glue-on googly eyes)

MAKING THE TURTLES

1 Cut five 10¹/₂in (26.5cm) squares from the water fabric, and one 11¹/₄in (28.5cm) square. Cut this larger square diagonally to make two half-square triangles.

2 Cut one 11¹/₄in (28.5cm) square of rock fabric, and cut it diagonally as you did with the larger water square.

3 Cut two border strips 7¹/₂x50¹/₂in (19x128cm), and two 7¹/₂x45in (19x114cm), all along the lengthwise grain of the fabric.

4 To prepare the IMA blocks, cut the following:

- twenty-eight 5¹/₂in (14cm) squares of water fabric
- sixteen 5¹/₂in (14cm) squares from the turtle shell fabric
- sixteen 4¹/₂in (11.5cm) squares from the turtle shell fabric
- four 5¹/₂in squares from the rock fabric
- sixteen curves (template A) from freezer paper
- sixteen backgrounds (template B) from freezer paper

5 Sew one water half-square triangle to one rock half-square triangle. Press towards the rock fabric. Repeat with the remaining triangles.

6 Press the sixteen freezer paper backgrounds onto the sixteen 5½in (14cm) shell squares. Press the sixteen freezer paper curves onto the sixteen smaller shell squares.

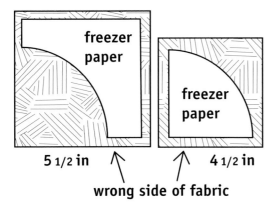

5 1/2 in   4 1/2 in

wrong side of fabric

7 Use method 1 (see page 24) to prepare these pieces for IMA. Be sure to clip the inner curves, but NOT the outer curves!

8 Pin two prepared shell curves onto two of the 5½in (14cm) squares of rock fabric. Pin two prepared shell backgrounds onto the other two 5½in (14cm) squares of rock fabric.

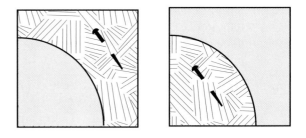

9 Pair up the remaining fourteen curves and fourteen backgrounds with a 5½in (14cm) water square. Set all these aside; DO NOT appliqué yet!

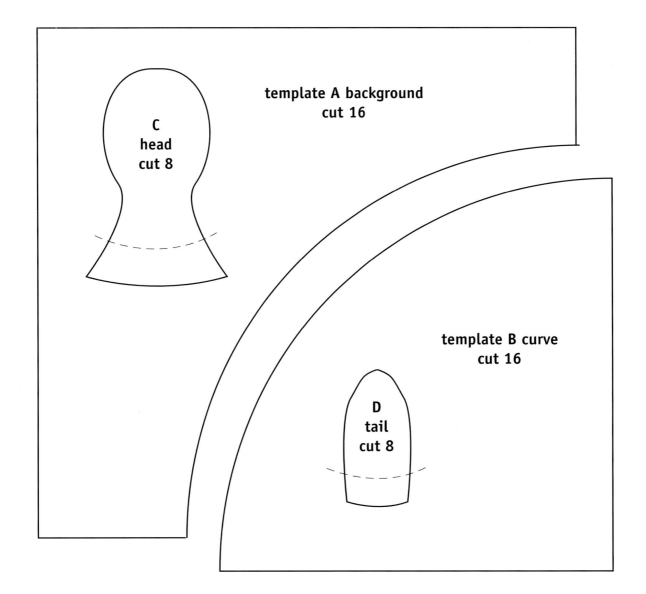

C
head
cut 8

**template A background
cut 16**

**template B curve
cut 16**

D
tail
cut 8

MAKING THE HEADS AND TAILS

1 Trace, cut and press eight freezer paper head shapes (template C) onto the reverse side of your chosen head fabric, and prepare using Method 1.

2 Trace, cut and press eight freezer paper tails (template D) onto the reverse side of your tail fabric, and prepare using method 4 (see page 30). The tails are going to be left three-dimensional.

leave outside of tail free

3 Turn the tails right side out and position each tail between a water square and a shell background: make eight of these. IMA around the curve, securing the raw end of the tail under the curve but leaving the rest of the tail free.

4 Place the prepared head shapes between the remaining water squares and shell backgrounds: pin them in position, remove shell backgrounds and IMA. Remove the freezer paper from behind the head shapes, add the background curve and IMA. Cut away all excess water fabric; remove the freezer paper and press.

5 Sew the different parts of each turtle block together, following the layout shown below; remember, though! – seven are on water backgrounds, and one is on the rock fabric.

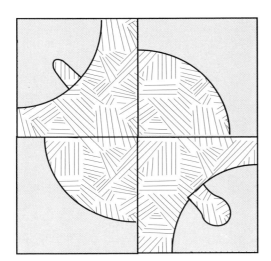

COMPLETING THE QUILT

1 Follow the diagram below to piece the quilt centre; alternate the turtle blocks with water blocks in the main part of the quilt, and add the extra rock squares and the 'turtle on the rocks' in the top left corner.

2 Embroider, glue or stitch on the eyes as appropriate.

3 Add the border strips to the edges of the quilt centre; stitch the side borders on first, then the top and bottom.

4 Add the wadding and backing fabric, then quilt the design as you wish – the water and rock fabrics provide you with some wonderful creative possibilities! Bind the edges of the quilt to finish it.

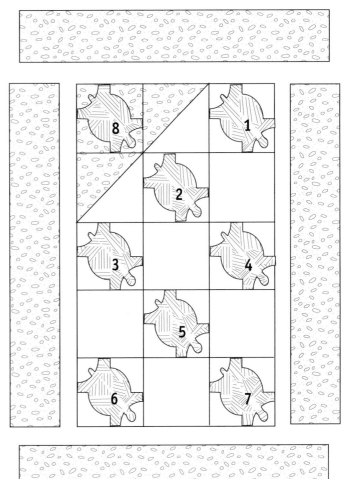

Antique Oak

Size: 72in (183cm) square; twenty-five 10in (25cm) blocks

SKILL LEVEL: *easy; no special skills needed*

TECHNIQUES REQUIRED:
*method 1, freezer paper and spray starch (see page 24),
or method 2 (see page 27)*

*A guilty conscience over an ever-growing collection of reproduction
antique fabrics led me to create a design which would showcase the
beauty of the fabrics and still be simple to stitch.*

*The oak leaf was a popular motif in 18th century quilts, but as
traditionally drawn it's rather fiddly. I simplified the curves and then
repeated the shape four times in an X-shaped layout.*

*A repeat block like this is a wonderful way to validate
your collection! Hand-dyed fabrics, plaids, large flower
patterns or novelty prints would all work beautifully
in this design (see the alternative colourway below).*

MATERIALS:

- 25 different fabrics for the oak leaves, 10in (25cm) square in each – or 1¼ yd (115cm) if you're using a single fabric for all the appliqué shapes
- 2yd (2m) neutral-coloured background fabric for the blocks
- 2¼ yd (a generous 2m) for the first and final borders, cut on the **lengthwise** grain of the fabric. (If you use a printed stripe fabric, as I did, you may need more fabric to match the print.)
- 2¼ yd (a generous 2m) for the accent strip in the border, and the binding; cut these also on the lengthwise grain
- One rotary-cut strip 2x40in (5x102cm) for the corners in the sashing (you could use the remainder of your accent strip if it suits your sashing fabric!)
- ⅞ yd (80cm) sashing fabric

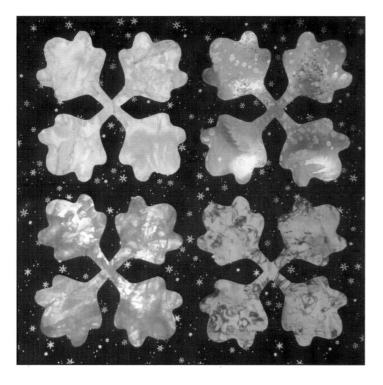

MAKING THE OAK LEAF BLOCKS

1 Trace the oak leaf shape on page 78 onto the freezer paper 25 times, and cut out these shapes.

To save time you could trace just five oak leaf shapes then layer four additional sheets of freezer paper under the originals; staple them together within the design area and cut out five at a time! Carefully undo the staples with a staple remover and you'll have your appliqué shapes ready in a fraction of the time.

2 Using method 1 or 2, whichever you prefer, use your oak leaf fabrics to prepare the leaf shapes for IMA.

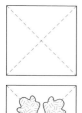

3 From your background fabric, cut twenty-five 10½in (26.5cm) squares. Finger-press each square diagonally into quarters and use these folds to help you centre your fabric shapes on the squares. IMA all 25 squares, then cut away the background fabric from behind the appliquéd shapes and remove the freezer paper.

MAKING THE QUILT TOP

1 Stitch alternate sashing strips and corner pieces together to make a narrow unit as shown; make four units like this in total.

x4

Antique Oak
template,
cut 25

2 Stitch alternate appliqué squares and sashing strips to make a wider unit as shown (right); make five units like this in total. The next task is to join the rows.

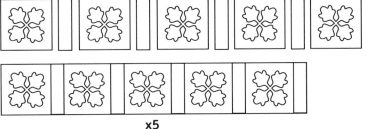

x5

3 Beginning with an appliqué/sashing row, and alternating wide and narrow units (**a**), stitch the rows together to construct the quilt top (**b**). Be sure to match your corner units to the vertical sashing strips above them for a perfect match.

CREATING THE BORDERS AND FINISHING THE QUILT

1 Follow the diagram below to cut and sew a border piece for each of the four edges of the quilt top. Press the seams of the accent fabric outwards as shown.

2 Mark the centre of each border strip with a pin; lay the border strips onto the quilt top, right sides together, matching the centres.

3 Stitch the borders to each edge of the quilt top, then mitre and IMA the corners of the borders. (See Mitred Borders on page 38 for more detailed instructions.)

4 Quilt the design as you wish. I first machine-quilted each block in the ditch, using my walking foot and a nylon thread. The quilt was then secured, and I could proceed to hand quilt each block without any further tacking!

5 Add the wadding and the backing fabric of your choice, and bind the quilt to finish it.

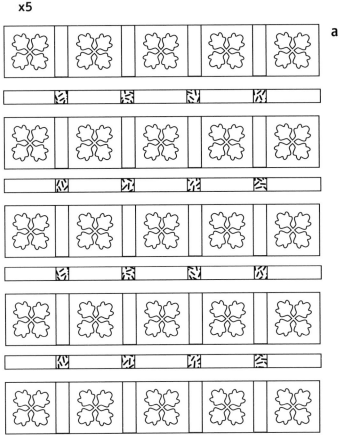

a

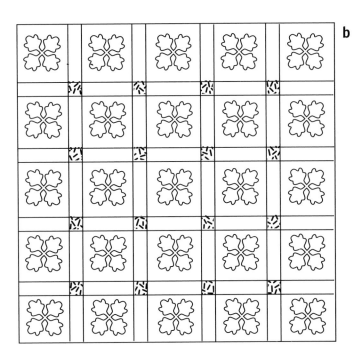

b

Dresden Plate Quilt

size: approximately 80x110in (200x280cm) – single bed size
fifteen 12in (30cm) blocks

SKILL LEVEL: *dedicated beginner, or intermediate*

TECHNIQUES REQUIRED:
method 3 (see page 28); basic rotary-cutting skills

The Dresden Plate design is the epitome of a traditional patchwork quilt, but it's often avoided because of its appliqué element. Now with Invisible Machine Appliqué you can easily create your very own heirloom.

Be sure to choose a varied selection of prints for your plates. Vary the tone and colours so that the plates will 'sing'! The example (right) is a detail of Liberty Dresden Plate 1 stitched by Cathy Corbishley Michel.

MATERIALS:

- ⅓yd (30cm) each of six 'wedge' fabrics
- ⅓yd (30cm) for centre circles
- 2yd (2m) background fabric plus 1½yd (1.5m) for lattice strips and nine-patch blocks – 3½yd (3.5m) in total
- 2yd (2m) contrast fabric for lattice strips and nine-patch blocks
- 1yd (1m) matching or contrasting fabric for straight strip binding (you'll need more if you want to bind the edge with bias strips)
- ¾yd (60cm) fabric for border one, pieced
- 1¼yd (1m) fabric for border two, pieced
- 2yd (1.6m) fabric for border three
- 2½yd (2.5m) featherweight iron-on interfacing

CREATING THE 'PLATES'

Cutting and sewing the wedges

1 Trace the wedge and circle shapes on page 83 and make a template of each one.

2 Decide which order you want your six wedge fabrics to appear in on the 'plates.' Lay the six fabrics on top of each other, in this order, on your ironing board; spray them with starch, and press them together (this helps the fabrics to keep their positions as you cut the shapes).

3 Carefully move this pile to your working surface and mark 30 wedge shapes on the top fabric (you can flip the pile over and mark on the wrong side of the fabric if it's easier to see the pencil markings that way); trace the shapes right next to each other as shown in the diagram.

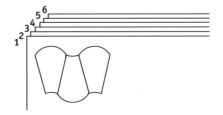

4 Use your ruler and rotary cutter to cut the shapes apart, then use the rotary cutter to cut the curves at each end of the wedge shapes. *Keep the fabrics in one pile, and in the same order, throughout this process.*

If you prefer, you could replace the interfacing squares with more squares of the circle fabric before you stitch – then turn them out but leave the backing fabric in place.

5 Sew each set of six wedges together in the same order. Press the seams to the right.

6 Sew two sets of six together to form a circle, pressing the final seams in the same direction as the others. Complete all the plates in the same way.

7 Using method 3 (lining with fusible interfacing, see page 28), cut 15 squares of featherweight interfacing 2in (5cm) larger all round than your sewn plates.

8 Place the 'nice' sides of one plate and one piece of interfacing together – this puts the glue side of the interfacing on your table top, and the wrong side of your pieced plate facing you. Using your shortest machine stitch, sew around the plate ¼in (5mm) in from the curved edge.

9 Trim very close to your stitching, then cut a small opening in the centre of the interfacing piece and turn the plate right side out through the opening. Carefully press just the edges of the interfacing to the wrong side of the plate and cut away the excess interfacing from the centre of the shape. Put this plate to one side and stitch the others in exactly the same way.

Adding the central circles

1 Cut fifteen 3in (7.5cm) squares of circle fabric and fifteen matching squares of interfacing. Place the 'nice' sides together – glue side to the table, wrong side of the fabric facing you.

2 Position the circle template in the centre of each square and draw round it. Insert a few pins round the edge of the circle and sew as before. Clip, turn out, press and trim the shapes as you did for the plates, then create all the other centre circles in the same way.

Assembling the plate blocks

1 Cut fifteen 12½in (31cm) squares of your background fabric. Fold each square into quarters and finger-press the folds.

2 Unfold the squares and use the folds to position a prepared plate centrally on each square. Position each plate either 'on seam' (**a**) or 'on wedge' (**b**), but make sure that each one is positioned in the same way.

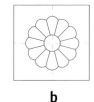

a   b

You may decide to put wedge 1 always in the same place (eg on the vertical fold), or to position the plates randomly on the squares. Lay the blocks out on the floor first and decide on the correct placing of each block. Believe me, it matters!

3 Put a pin in each wedge to hold the shape, then IMA each of the plates in position. Pin a prepared circle over the exact centre of each plate shape and IMA .

4 Carefully cut away the background fabric from behind each central circle and plate shape.

CUTTING AND SEWING THE SASHING SECTIONS

1 Cut thirty-two 2in (5cm) strips of contrast fabric: call these strips D (for dark). Cut twenty 2in (5cm) strips of background fabric: call these strips L (for light).

2 Sew three strips of D and L together in this order: LDL (**c**). Press the seams to the dark fabric. Sub-cut these units into 2in (5cm) sections (**d**), to create a total of forty-eight LDL sections.

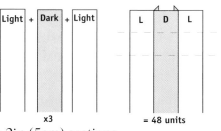

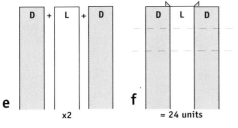

e x2 f = 24 units

3 Sew two strips of D and one of L together in this order: DLD (**e**). Press the seams to the dark fabric. Sub-cut these units into 2in (5cm) sections (**f**) for a total of twenty-four DLD sections.

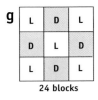

g

24 blocks

4 Sew the LDLs and the DLDs into nine-patch units as shown (**g**), to create a total of twenty-four nine-patch blocks.

5 Stitch the remaining strips together in units of three in this order: DLD (**h**). Press the seams to the dark fabric. Sub-cut these strips into thirty-eight 12½in (31cm) lengths.

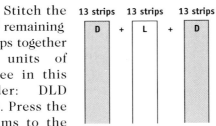

13 strips   13 strips   13 strips

D + L + D

h

You now have:
  15 appliquéd blocks (**i**)
  38 DLD striped rectangles (**j**)
  24 nine-patch blocks (**k**)

k

i   j

ASSEMBLING THE QUILT TOP
Completing the piecing

1 Following the diagram on page 84, lay all the pieces out in the correct positions. Piece the quilt top together row by row.

ROW 1 (below): 9-patch, horizontal DLD, 9-patch, horizontal DLD etc

ROW 2 (below): vertical DLD, plate block, vertical DLD, plate block etc

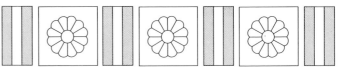

ROWS 3, 5, 7, 9, 11: as row 1

ROWS 4, 6, 8, 10: as row 2
Once all the rows are stitched, join the rows in the correct order to complete the piecing.

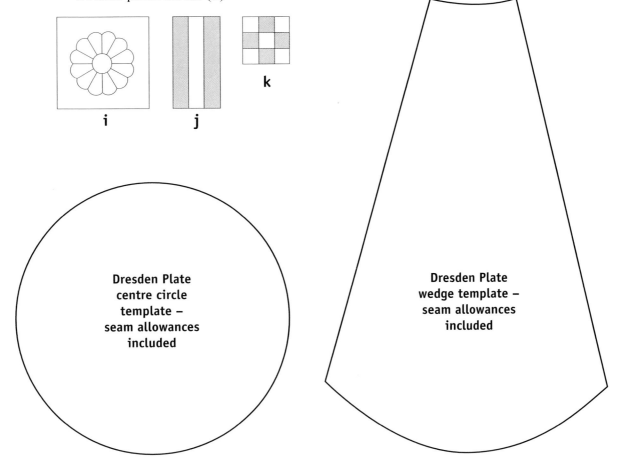

Dresden Plate centre circle template – seam allowances included

Dresden Plate wedge template – seam allowances included

Border 1   Border 2   Border 3

Adding the borders

BORDER 1 is 2¹/₂in (6.5cm) wide when finished. From your ³/₄yd (60cm) of fabric cut seven strips 3in (7.5cm) wide. Piece these strips together, then cut to fit.

BORDER 2 is 4¹/₂in (11.5cm) wide when finished. From your 1¹/₄yd (1m) of fabric cut eight strips 5in (12.5cm) wide. Piece these strips together, then cut to fit.

BORDER 3 is 6¹/₂in (16.5cm) wide when finished. From your 2yd (160cm) of fabric cut nine strips 7in (17.5cm) wide. Piece these strips together, then cut to fit.

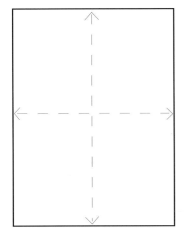

Remember always to measure across the centre of your pieced quilt top to obtain the correct measurements for making your borders. Edges of quilt tops stretch; if you make a border to fit a stretched edge your quilt will never lie properly flat. Mitre the corners or set the borders straight – the choice is yours.

FINISHING

Quilting

I chose to quilt this design by hand within the plate block. I machine-quilted the lattice sashing and the nine-patch blocks with straight lines, working in the ditch with YLI Wonder thread in the top and Heirloom in the bobbin. After more than ten years of regular use at home and in class the quilt is still in perfect condition.

Shown below is the template I used for the hand-quilting. As an alternative you could fill in the background of the plates with echo quilting or cross-hatching, or just outline the plates and the block ¹/₄in (5mm) from the edges (see right). Some shops stock a ¹/₄in-wide masking tape which is perfect for outlining shapes so that you can stitch at a consistent distance.

Binding

I seldom use bias binding as I feel it stretches, and also takes so very much time to prepare. See the general instructions (page 48) on how to bind a straight edge, and how to do mitred binding in a jiffy!

Psychedelic Skippy

Size: *20x12in (50.5x30cm)*

SKILL LEVEL: *easy*

TECHNIQUES REQUIRED:
*method 1, freezer paper and spray starch (see page 24);
stained glass appliqué*

*This kangaroo is not a traditional stained glass appliqué in
the true sense; to be honest he's a big ol' cheat, but so
what?! He's cute, I love him and he's a good project for
someone working with prepared bias tape for the first time.*

*The Aboriginal fabric in the background and the eucalyptus
backing were gifts long ago from a 'travelling Australian' and dear
friend, Catherine Combe. But if no Aussies are currently crossing
your path, choose any exciting background and a hand-dyed-look
fabric for the kangaroo, then make your own Skippy in a jiffy!*

PREPARING SKIPPY

1 Using a pencil, trace all the lines from the full-size Skippy pattern (page 88-89) onto your freezer paper. Cut out the paper shape, cutting along the outside lines ONLY (**a**).

2 Place the paper kangaroo shape waxy side down onto the right side of your chosen kangaroo fabric and press with a hot, dry iron (**b**).

3 Once the shape is secured, leave the freezer paper in place and use a pencil or fabric maker to draw all round the outside edges of Skippy (**c**).

4 Move to your cutting mat and gently lift the tail section of the freezer paper away from the fabric. Cut along the edge between A and B shown with a = mark on the drawing.

Gently pat the freezer paper down into position again and, with a fabric pen or pencil, draw along the edge of B onto the fabric (**d**). Each line you draw will eventually be covered by bias binding; **don't** cut your kangaroo fabric.

5 Repeat the process of removing sections of freezer paper, drawing and pressing until only your kangaroo fabric remains with pencil lines defining its limbs. Remove the remaining freezer paper (**e**).

6 Carefully cut your fabric Skippy out along his outer edges ONLY.

7 Very gently, place Skippy in the centre of your background fabric (**f**). Pin your kangaroo down, sport, then he's ready for the bias binding.

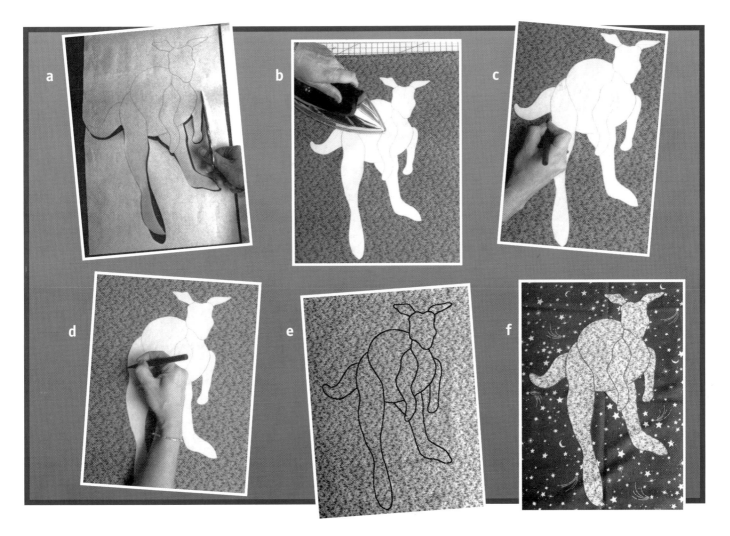

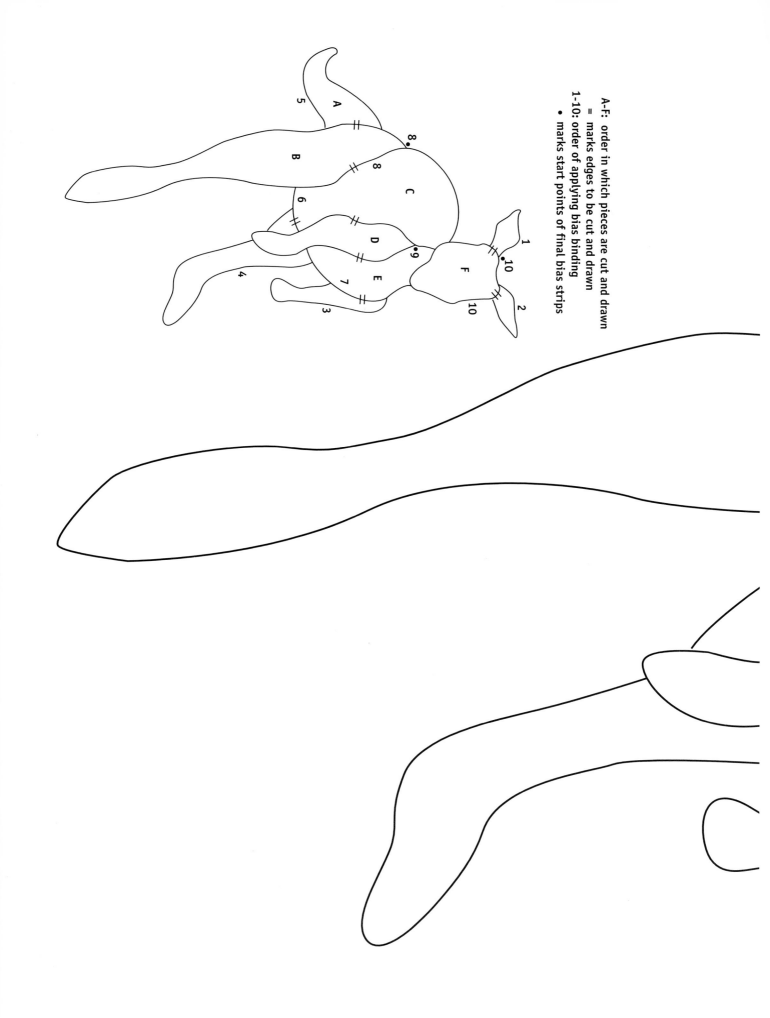

A-F: order in which pieces are cut and drawn
= marks edges to be cut and drawn
1-10: order of applying bias binding
• marks start points of final bias strips

ADDING THE BIAS BINDING

The bias binding I've recommended has a fusible strip on the reverse side protected by a white paper strip. You remove the paper, cut the strip and lay it in position. Then press it with a medium hot iron and it's firmly fused in place awaiting your stitches to secure it permanently.

The small Skippy pattern (page 88) has numbers on the lines which show you the order in which the pieces of binding are stitched on. You must always position, secure and stitch one piece of binding before you proceed to any piece which goes over it.

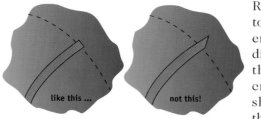

like this ...   not this!

Remember to trim each end in the direction of the line it crosses, as shown on the left.

This also may be a good place to use the smoke-coloured invisible thread that I mentioned earlier. It seems to blend even better into the blackness of the bias binding and, if you keep your straight stitches very close to the edge of the tape they will blend into the shadow of the binding ... even on a light-coloured fabric!

1 Measure your first bias strip – the piece which goes round Skippy's right ear. Trim it and press it in place over the exposed edge of the fabric. Coax the strip into the most pleasing curves you can manage – as long as they cover the edge of your kangaroo.

2 IMA the inside curve of the binding first, then IMA the outside curve. There's no need to backstitch here as the ends of the first strips will be covered by subsequent ones!

3 Once strips numbered 1-5 are in position you will do 6 and 7, which will cover the ends of 3 and 4.

4 Strips numbered 8, 9 and 10 are finishing strips. Begin stitching these at the dots shown on the diagram. The raw end at the beginning of the bias strip will eventually be covered when the circuit round each shape is complete.

QUILTING AND FINISHING

For the design shown in the opening photograph, I machine-quilted Skippy using a variegated Sulky thread. I free-form quilted the background, following the lines on the fabric. Then a simple binding was all that was needed to finish off my Trippy Skippy!

I sincerely hope that you've enjoyed the techniques and projects that I've shown you. As a teacher I'm always delighted to see any works I may have inspired. If you make one of these quilts, or use IMA to help you complete a design of your own, I'd love to have a photograph of the finished project!

Please bring it along to any of the shows where I'm demonstrating, or to any classes you're taking with me. I'm now in the process of preparing

INNOVATIONS IN INVISIBLE MACHINE APPLIQUÉ (BOOK 2), and I assure you that your input would be most valuable.

To contact me personally or to enquire about lectures or classes please write to me at my e-mail address:

IMA_dawn@hotmail.com

Happy appliqué!

Try to Remember … quilt by Dawn Cameron-Dick

What lies behind us and what lies before us
are tiny matters, compared to what lies within us.

RALPH WALDO EMERSON

Resources

Most of the supplies suggested in this book are available from any good quilt shop. If you should have difficulty locating any item you can be sure to get it from one of the suppliers listed below. But always try and support your local quilt shop, if possible!

YLI threads supplied by:

Quilt Direct, Iliffe House, Iliffe Avenue, Oadby, Leicester LE2 5LS
(ring 0116 271 0033 or fax 0116 271 0099 for a free
full-colour brochure; e-mail: enquiries@quiltdirect.co.uk
or check the web on: www.quiltdirect.co.uk)

IMA distribution inquiries for Australia and North America:

Quilters' Resource Inc., PO Box 148850, Chicago, IL 60614
(telephone 1-773-278-5695 or fax 1-773-278-1348
or e-mail: info@quiltersresource.com)

Sewing machines and technical advice:

World of Sewing, 56-64 Camden Road, Royal Tunbridge Wells, Kent TN1 2QP
(telephone 01892 536314, fax 01892 520810,
e-mail: richard@sewing-world.co.uk)

Quilt photography by:

Steve Sullivan (01892 654309); commissions and assignments undertaken.

Machine quilting on *Into the Deep End* and *Antique Oak* by:
Mandy Shaw (01323 845297)

OTHER TITLES AVAILABLE FROM TEAMWORK CRAFTBOOKS

Stained Glass Patchwork by Gail Lawther
An introduction to this simple technique, with colour photographs
of 15 projects, and a 10-page pattern library   ISBN 0 9532590 0 5

Quirky Quilts by Dorothy Stapleton
Dorothy introduces some of her humorous quilts, plus projects based
on her crazy patchwork techniques   ISBN 0 9532590 1 3

A Trip Around the World by Gail Lawther
25 patchwork, quilting and appliqué projects inspired by different countries,
plus over 20 pages of extra motifs for inspiration   ISBN 0 9532590 3 x

Confessions of a Quilter by Dorothy Stapleton
Clever tricks, time-saving tips, and how to turn stitching disasters
into design features!   ISBN 0 9532590 4 8